Boston /Architecture

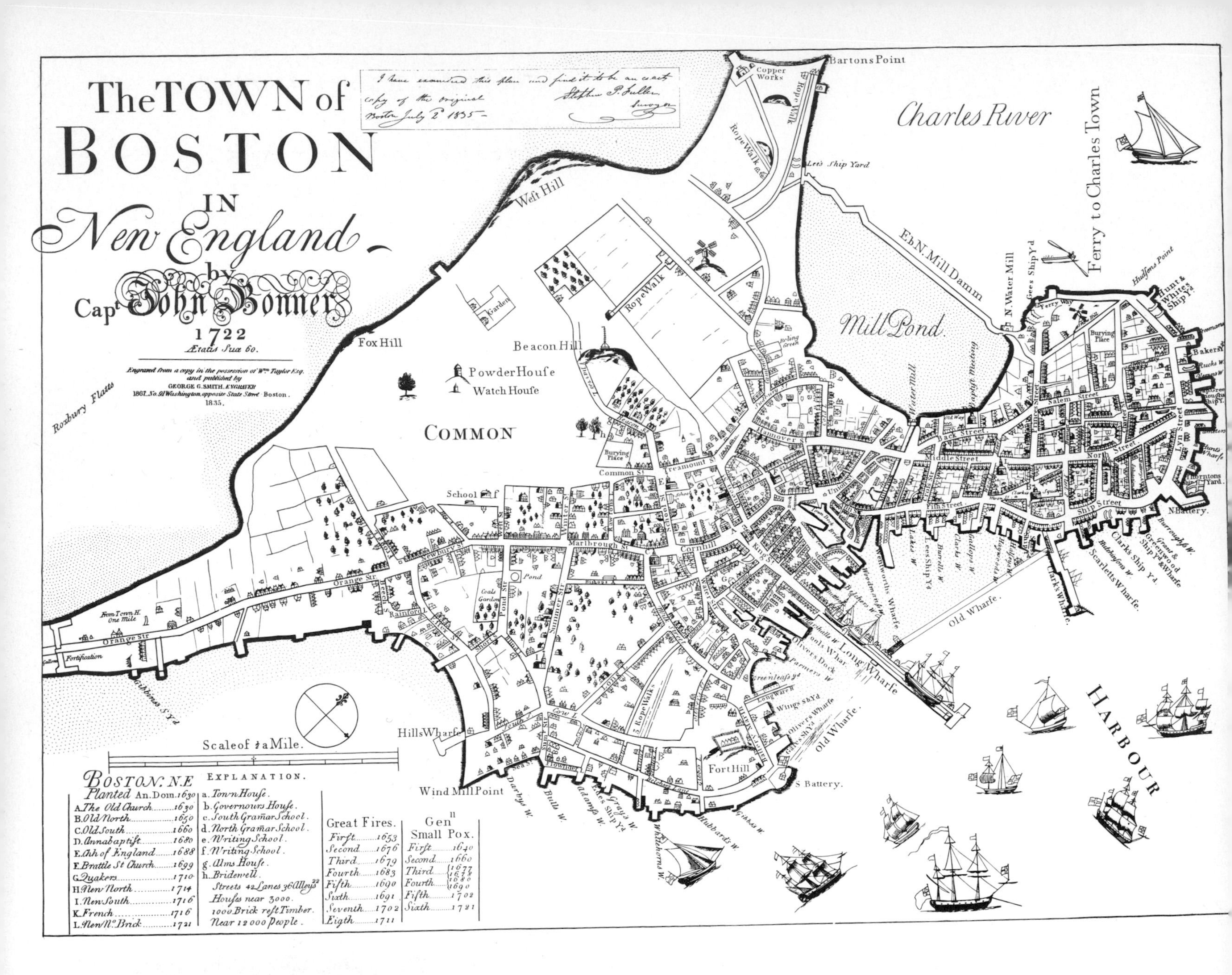

photography Nanette Sexton
Richard Rogers
Todd Stuart

research Marjorie Prager

graphics Anne Meyer

production Freeman/Hardenbergh Associates

The Boston Society of Architects
a chapter of the
American Institute of Architects

produced and edited
Donald Freeman

The MIT Press
Cambridge, Massachusetts
and London, England

Boston Architecture

Second printing, April 1971

Set in Linotype Helvetica and
printed at The Nimrod Press, Boston

ISBN 0 262 02070 X (hardcover)
ISBN 0 262 52015 X (paperback)
Library of Congress catalog card number: 72-122927

Contents

Acknowledgments

Boston/Architecture developed from a series of discussions started in 1968 by a committee of architects, Donald C. Freeman, Charles G. Hilgenhurst, Thomas F. McNulty, and William J. Geddis, Chairman, who had been designated by the Boston Society of Architects and asked to develop a program for the 102nd Annual Convention of the American Institute of Architects to be held in Boston in June 1970.

It was agreed that a book on Boston's architecture, written by architects, would be one of the important contributions to the Convention, if it were significant and avoided the usual guidebook format. And so the work began.

A grant of five thousand dollars from the Boston Society of Architects provided the initial funding for this work, and special credit must go to the then President, Joseph P. Richardson, FAIA, and his directors for their confidence in the idea and also to past President John W. Peirce, FAIA, and President Hugh A. Stubbins Jr., FAIA, for their subsequent support.

Committee Member Donald C. Freeman offered the services of his firm, Freeman/Hardenbergh Associates, to undertake the research, writing, photography, graphics, and assembling of the work, and a contract with the firm was effected.

John Coolidge, Professor of Fine Arts at Harvard University, because of his unique knowledge of cities—Boston in particular—was asked to write an introduction. The M.I.T. Press had confidence in the concept and agreed to the publication of the book.

We give special acknowledgment to sponsors, as their financial support provided the only means by which the first publication of the book could be realized:

Johns Manville Corp., New York City
Aberthaw Construction Company, Boston, Mass.
Electric Council of New England and participating member companies:
- Boston Edison Company
- Brockton Edison Company
- Central Maine Power Company
- Central Vermont Public Service Corporation
- Citizens Utilities Company (Newport Division)
- Concord Electric Company
- Exeter & Hampton Electric Company
- Fall River Electric Light Company
- Fitchburg Gas & Electric Light Company
- Green Mountain Power Corporation
- Maine Public Service Company
- New England Electric System
- New England Gas & Electric Association
- Newport Electric Corporation
- Public Service Company of New Hampshire

Macomber Construction Company, Boston, Mass.
Bolt Beranek & Newman, Cambridge, Mass.
Wescott Construction Company, Attleboro, Mass.
New England Mutual Life Insurance Company, Boston, Mass.
Massachusetts State Association of Architects
- Western Massachusetts Chapter
- Central Massachusetts Chapter
- Boston Society of Architects

Others contributed their time and judgment to this work, among them: Mrs. Lester Werman; Charles R. Strickland, FAIA, with his vast knowledge of the city and its people; Clifford Douglas Stewart; and, of course, no account of Boston would be complete without the advice and inspiration of Walter Muir Whitehill, Director of the Boston Atheneum, from whose work *Boston—A Topographical History* we borrow extensively.

We, as architects, hope this book will serve the student and visitor in identifying the spaces and buildings, both old and new, which are part of our heritage.

William J. Geddis, AIA
Host Chapter Chairman
Boston Society of Architects

Introduction

John Coolidge

The illustrations in this book direct attention to what is visually remarkable in Boston, be it the excellent, the appalling, or the unique. The accompanying text provides background. But these do not aim to record experience; they seek to stimulate it. The viewer-reader must go out, see for himself, and draw his own conclusions. This introduction offers a few historical generalizations in the hope of encouraging him to make some comprehensive judgments.

Boston's conservatism is a reality, at least if one evaluates its best buildings by an international standard. In achitecture, the principal old cities of the United States are like the actors in an inbred stock company; they change their costumes but never their characters. Philadelphia is the first to give form to major ideas from Europe, whether in William Penn's plan, Latrobe's romantic classicism, or Lescaze's international style. New York, faultlessly suave and faintly tired, restates the internationally accepted clichés a little late in the day, as at Mangin's City Hall, Upjohn's Trinity Church, McKim's Low Library, and Mies's Seagram building. Chicago fosters innovations: the balloon frame, skyscraper construction, and the prairie house. And Boston? Boston, like Oxford, has never blushed to be the last place

to work seriously in an outworn tradition. The very outrageousness of its conservatism can occasionally, eventually, and mysteriously inspire the creation of new values. At the Paul Revere house, folk Gothic survived into the age of Bernini; yet it is from such modest seventeenth-century buildings that the shingle style took off. To Mid-Atlantic patrons of advanced taste the "toothpick colonial" of Bulfinch and his followers must have seemed a symbol of Federalist reaction; yet for twentieth-century urbanists of all persuasions their work is a model of civilized restraint. Perhaps just because Richardson's assertive use of masonry was so backward for its time, it is so sympathetic to our own. Does all this explain how Harvard could commission a full-blooded Georgian reproduction more than thirty years after it had appointed Gropius professor of architecture?

The book suggests a second trait. Boston has long had a partiality for established architects and has frequently imported them or their designs. Peter Harrison dispatched from Newport the drawings for King's Chapel and Christ Church; McKim and Johnson created and extended the Public Library; Gropius and Le Corbusier worked for Harvard, Aalto and Saarinen for M.I.T. But Boston has had little success in attracting gifted young men from other parts of the country. May the competition for the City Hall prove as much a breakthrough now

as the competition for Trinity Church was a century ago!

In 1899 Boston had almost as many commuters as New York and Chicago combined, and it was the first among American cities, as Daniel Burnham noted in 1909, to realize "the advantages of cooperation between the great city and the outlying districts." After World War II the tide began to turn. Executives still commute from Brookline but often now outward to their offices, just as scientists commute outward from Cambridge to the electronic laboratories. One result was the establishment, in 1964, of the Massachusetts Bay Transportation Authority, the first such authority in the country to be regional in scope and to include all modes of travel. Other results of commuting, whether inward or outward, are clearly recorded in the photographs in this book. The face of the central city has been scarred by the effects, first, of flight, then of blight, and now of urban renewal—a familiar tale, but happily, in Boston's case, only half the story. With rare exceptions Burnham's "outlying districts" are neither independent entities nor havens for escapists. From the founding of Cambridge in 1630 to the establishment of the industrial parks along Route 128 in our own day, Boston has created these out-of-town communities as specialized complements to the central city. The peculiar relationship is expressed politically by the fact that there has never been any strong or lasting urge to amalgamate. Today, the mayor of Boston is responsible for a smaller portion of "his" metropolis than any comparable executive except that ceremonial personage the lord mayor of London.

Architecturally, this situation results in an unusual diffusion of interest. Recognizing this, the authors have included Cambridge within the scope of this work. It was not practical to go further, which is unfortunate, for the mills and mill housing along the Merrimack relate to Boston exactly as Pullman does to Chicago. The colonial and federal mansions of Medford and Waltham, the girdle of Richardsonian suburbs from Quincy in the south all the way around to Malden in the north, the Breuer and the Gropius houses in Lincoln—all these are an integral part of the architecture of Boston, illuminating its successes and essential to the understanding of its failures.

Commuting out is no more important than commuting away. Boston–New York is the second most heavily traveled airlane in the country. If half the local intellectuals admire Boston as a stubborn survival, for the other half it is the northern anchor of the first true megalopolis. This has meant a decline in regional economic independence. Lever Brothers moved its headquarters to New York; Time Incorporated gobbled up Little, Brown. On the other hand, the evolution of the megalopolis has brought increasing specialization and increasing eminence within the fields of speciality. Yale has moved its investments from Wall Street to State Street; the Massachusetts General was recently voted the finest hospital in the country; and Adlai Stevenson, no less, paid wry tribute to "the rigors to your climate and your classrooms." Boston has to live increasingly by its wits.

In building, the story is similar but more complex. Between the two world wars local architecture sank to the lowest level in the

settlement's history. During these decades the best-known Boston architects were best known precisely for their work outside Boston: Cram for St. John the Divine, the Shepley office for The New York Hospital, Perry, Shaw, and Hepburn for Colonial Williamsburg. This deplorable situation was transformed by outsiders, in the first instance by men who were brought by a succession of inspired deans to teach at the M.I.T. and Harvard architectural schools. Business followed, as when the Prudential asked an architect from California to design its local branch. Then came new buildings for the universities and finally for the various levels of government. Today, Boston and adjacent parts of New England have become a dispersed architectural museum. In one day a tourist could see representative examples of the work of Richardson, Wright, Gropius, LeCorbusier, Breuer, Aalto, Nervi, Saarinen, and a host of other eminent architects; it would be an eclectic tour, perhaps—a strenuous tour, certainly—but one hard to rival anywhere else in the world.

If contemporary Boston has taken, it also gives and has given. One can point to the popularity of its professional schools and to the fact that now, for the first time, several local firms have a truly international practice. Is the city becoming more influential as it grows more provincial? Is the Athens of America turning into the Florence of the United States?

Beacon Hill
1

commercial
street
fitzgerald
epressway
hanover
street
14•
blossom
street
merrimac
street
street
16•
chardon
street
new
new
sudbury
street
cambridge
street
9•
bowdoin
street
n. market
street
s. market
street
avenue
new atlantic
street
court
street
state
2•
7•
6•
1•
street
17•
11•
mount
vernon
8•
12•
5•
•15
street
chestnut
3•
4•
13•
10•
street
beacon
street
park
milk
street
congress
street
street
street
franklin
street
street
drive
storrow
street
charles
washington
street
expressway
fitzgerald
avenue
federal
atlantic
street
tremont
street
street
street
arlington
boylston
berkeley
clarendon
street
summer
avenue
washington
avenue
street
kneeland
street
street
stuart
columbus
harrison
new dorchester
street

Beacon Hill

1. ▸ State House
Beacon and Park Streets
Charles Bulfinch; 1795-98
Rear Extension: Charles E. Brigham; 1889–95
Wings: R. Clipston Sturgis; 1916

2. ▸ Louisburg Square
Mount Vernon Street to Pinckney Street
Plan: S. P. Fuller; 1826
Constructed: 1834–37

◂ 3. Sears House (now Somerset Club)
42 Beacon Street
Alexander Parris; 1818

4. ▸ Women's City Club
39–40 Beacon Street
Probably Alexander Parris; 1818

◂ 5. 13–17 Chestnut Street
Charles Bulfinch; c. 1805

◂ 6. 57 Mount Vernon Street
Charles Bulfinch; pre-1807

7. ▸ Second Harrison Grey Otis House
85 Mount Vernon Street
Charles Bulfinch; 1800

8. ▶ 9 West Cedar Street
Asher Benjamin; 1833

◀ 9. Saint John the Evangelist
35 Bowdoin Street
possibly Solomon Willard; 1831

◀ 10. Third Harrison Grey Otis House
45 Beacon Street
Charles Bulfinch; 1806

11. ▶ Charles Street Universalist Meeting House
70 Charles Street
probably Asher Benjamin; 1804

12. Acorn Street

13. Branch Street

◀ 14. Charles River Park
West End
Victor Gruen & Associates; 1958–

◀ 15. 70–72 Mount Vernon Street (apartments)
(originally Thayer Brothers Double House)
Probably Richard M. Upjohn; c. 1840
Second use: Boston University School of Theology
Chestnut Street Addition: Bellows & Aldrich and James A. Holt Associates; 1917–18
Interior renovations into apartments: Bullerjahn Associates; 1965

16. ▶ Bulfinch Pavilion
Massachusetts General Hospital
Charles Bulfinch; 1816–17

17. Boston Athenaeum
10½ Beacon Street
Edward Cabot and George Dexter; 1847

Beacon Hill

In the minds of many people, Boston has been epitomized in the personality of a straight-laced, snobbish maiden aunt whose ancestors arrived on the *Mayflower,* who scorned bad manners, was outraged by banned books, and who avoided confrontation with those whose lives were slightly less perfect than her own. The image of the city has softened, grown younger and more tolerant over the years, but what was perhaps the heart of that prudish old lady—Beacon Hill—has been preserved, if only externally. To tourists not privileged to see beyond the gracious façades of the houses of Louisburg Square or the quaintness of the Charles Street antique shops, the heart of Boston's image appears never to have missed a beat.

Originally known as Sentry Hill—a pasture ground where cattle and horses grazed—this part of the Shawmut peninsula was the choice of Boston's first settler, William Blaxton. According to Walter Whitehill, "he built a house, planted an orchard, and lived in solitary peace with his vegetables, flowers and books, until the autumn of 1630, when his quiet was rudely interrupted by the arrival of settlers of the Massachusetts Bay Colony." For more than a hundred years this area remained a sunny slope with abundant fresh water upon which the early Bostonians chose to build their estates.

Beacon Hill was the central peak of the Trimountain, a landmark which rose above the main part of the Shawmut peninsula; the ridge's other two peaks, Pemberton and Mount Vernon, have completely disappeared, and Beacon Hill itself has lost about sixty feet from its original height. Mount Vernon, more commonly known at that time as Mount Whoredom, was from the outset a thorn in the side of those who inhabited the utterly respectable south slope of Beacon Hill. The major development began in 1795 when an

TOW ZONE
NO PARKING
ANY TIME
STREET CLEANING
TUE. & FRI.

organization known as the Mount Vernon Proprietors leveled Mount Whoredom, simultaneously using the gravel they removed to fill the Charles River along the line that is now Charles Street. Lots were subdivided and building began. The area lost much of its remote, rural quality when, in the same year, construction began on the State House, designed by Bulfinch. Land continued to be removed from Beacon Hill, and by 1824 it was lowered to its present height.

Building boomed for five years, and the character of the two slopes of the Hill was becoming more and more established. Building restrictions of what now seem a slightly eccentric nature were set; demands were made for passageways between houses to be wide enough for a cow to pass through, high enough for a boy with a basket on his head to pass under. S. P. Fuller, inspired by an earlier plan by Bulfinch for a garden square, drew up his idea for Louisburg Square in 1826. His plan was accepted, and the Square was to become the most fashionable, sought-after residential section in all of Boston. The lots were sold in 1834, and another building boom ensued, stopped only by the panic of 1837. By 1845 the period of major development was over.

Beginning in 1860 the newly filled Back Bay began to challenge Beacon Hill's supremacy as the city's most fashionable and impressive residential quarter. Beacon Hill refused to bend an inch to entice back any of those who drifted away and clung stubbornly to its old-established ways. Houses, however, fell into neglect, and the insidious process of conversion of single-family dwellings into rooming houses and flats began. Migration to the Back Bay was strongest from 1875 to 1880 and property values on Beacon Hill declined sharply, reaching their lowest ebb in 1905. Oliver Wendell Holmes in the 1870's had described Beacon Street as "the sunny street that holds the sifted few," but the appearance of stores, private schools, rooming houses and apartments indicated that the sifting process had reversed itself.

The turn of the century brought with it a turn of events, and old houses on the Hill were "rediscovered," refitted, and reclaimed. The family names that had disappeared to the Back Bay suddenly returned, but this time represented by members of a younger generation. The south slope of the Hill soon resumed its former prominence as the best of residential areas. Robert Shackleton wrote in *The Book of Boston* (1917): "Beacon Hill, the height of exclusiveness, the citadel of aristocracy, all this it has long been, as if its being a hill aided in giving it literal unapproachableness. It still retains its prideful poise, in its outward and visible signs of perfectly cared-for houses and correctness of dress and manners and equipage."

The revival of interest in Beacon Hill was so intense that it spread down to the river, engulfing parts of the neighborhood that had earlier been dismissed as suitable only for servants' quarters. Land valuation increased dramatically; for example, a house in Louisburg Square that was worth $14,800 in 1910 rose in price to $24,000 in 1920, to $34,000 in 1931, and costs about $140,000 today.

Beacon Hill was named for a warning

beacon that was set on its summit in 1634. A reproduction of the beacon was later presented to the Commonwealth, and its fate has been less happy than that of the area named for it. Walter Whitehill had this to say about the plight of the replica of the original beacon: "When accepted by the Commonwealth, the new monument stood in an agreeable little park. Today it resembles a cormorant perched on a spar buoy in a sea of parked cars, many of whose occupants doubtless think of it chiefly as an obstacle to traffic."

In 1955 Beacon Hill was created a historic district by act of the Massachusetts legislature and in 1963 was designated as a Registered National Historic Landmark by the Department of the Interior. The boundaries of the district have twice been enlarged so that today the external appearances of buildings between Beacon and Cambridge Streets, from Bowdoin Street to the Charles River are protected from thoughtless and inappropriate alteration. Occasional controversy arises about this overall preservation. In the early sixties there was a proposal to demolish the Thayer Mansion on Mount Vernon Street and its neo-Gothic addition fronting on Chestnut Street. These buildings were to be replaced with a multi-story apartment tower in the center of the block and low buildings, conforming to their Bulfinch neighbors, fronting on both streets. With community pressure against the project growing, the owner finally withdrew his application and converted the existing buildings into luxury apartments.

The attraction of Beacon Hill still lies in its architecture, which is miraculously well preserved. There is a great variety of styles united by a common human scale. The unifying brick of both walks and buildings turns out, on close inspection, to be made up of a wide range of colors. There is diversity of form also in the doorways, windows, and ironwork. To the tourist who sees only the street façade and delights in this amazing variety of detail and texture in the building materials, Beacon Hill is a slice of nineteenth-century life transfixed, an island of calm in the midst of the furor of the new Boston. But many of the twentieth-century inhabitants of the area are not living in the past; they have created within the old houses on both the south and north slopes of the Hill a younger and less "establishment" lifestyle. Charles Street, once only the home of antique shops and elegant florists, is now the meeting ground between the new and the old Bostonian, the hippy and the dowager, the young professional and the old guard. The issue of establishing a historic district is still open to debate; but while the controversy goes on, Beacon Hill has maintained a human scale and human quality that appear to be missing from the new Boston.

Back Bay

19

mount vernon street
charles street
tremont street
arlington street
berkeley street
clarendon street
dartmouth street
exeter street
fairfield street
gloucester street
hereford street
massachusetts avenue
storrow drive
beacon street
marlborough street
commonwealth avenue
newbury street
boylston street
massachusetts turnpike
huntington avenue
columbus avenue
tremont street
washington street
1
2
3
4
5
6
7
8
9
10
11
12
13
14
15
16
17
18
19
20
21
22
23
24
25

Back Bay

1. ▶ Arlington Street Subway Station
Arlington and Boylston Streets
Cambridge Seven Associates; 1968

2. ▶ First Lutheran Church in Boston
299 Berkeley Street
Pietro Belluschi; 1957

3. ▶ 180 Beacon Street (sculpture garden)
Carol R. Johnson; 1967

◀ 4. 330 Beacon Street (apartments)
Hugh Stubbins & Associates; 1960

◀ 5. Trinity Church
Copley Square
H. H. Richardson; 1874–77

◀ 6. Trinity Church Rectory
233 Clarendon Street
H. H. Richardson; 1879
3rd Story added; 1893

7. ▶ Prudential Center
Charles Luckman & Associates; 1965–

8. ▶ Boston Architectural Center
320 Newbury Street
Ashley Myer & Associates; 1967

9. John Hancock Tower
John Hancock Place
I. M. Pei & Partners; 1973

◀ **10.** Bonwit Teller
(originally Museum of Natural History)
Berkeley and Boylston Streets
William G. Preston; 1862

◀ **11.** Public Garden
c. 1900

◀ **12.** The Fenway
Frederick Law Olmsted; c. 1900

13. ▶ Arlington Street Church
Arlington and Boylston Streets
Arthur Gilman; 1859–61

14. ▶ Church of the Covenant
67 Newbury Street
Richard M. Upjohn; 1865–67

◀ **15.** Boston Public Library
Copley Square
McKim, Mead & White; 1887
Addition: Philip Johnson; 1971

◀ **16.** First Baptist Church (originally New Brattle Square Church)
Clarendon Street and Commonwealth Avenue
H. H. Richardson; 1870–72

17. First Church in Boston (Unitarian)
64 Marlborough Street
Ware and Van Brunt; 1865–67

◀ **18.** New Old South Church
Boylston and Dartmouth Streets
Cummings and Sears; 1874

19. ▶ Symphony Hall
Huntington and Massachusetts Avenues
McKim, Mead & White; 1900

20. ▶ Horticultural Hall
Huntington and Massachusetts Avenues
Wheelwright and Haven; 1901

21. ▶ Copley Square; 1883
Redesign: Sasaki, Dawson & Demay; 1969

22. Christian Science Church Center
I. M. Pei & Partners; 1970–

23. ▶ John F. Andrew House
32 Hereford Street
McKim, Mead and White; 1884–88

◀ **24.** G. A. Nickerson House
303 Commonwealth Avenue
McKim, Mead and White; 1895

25. B. W. Crowninshield House
164 Marlborough Street
H. H. Richardson; 1870–

Back Bay from the State House late 1850s

c. 1875

Back Bay

The Back Bay presents a multitude of conflicting images. The carefully scaled houses of the nineteenth century sit next to high-rise buildings that bear disconcertingly little relationship to them; the once elegant town houses are broken into flats and filled with students and secretaries; the well-kept front yards and polished brass doorplates are plagued by weeds and tarnish. The desire to rehabilitate the area as an in-town residential district has always been strong, but there are economic pressures to change its character and scale. In 1970, a new zoning envelope was established with a taskforce of architects, planners, lawyers, historians and business men advising the City. It recognized the importance of limiting new high-rise construction to a narrow spine following the Boylston Street and Massachusetts turnpike extension line. Strong community support of this policy was indicative of a new resolve to preserve the scale and character from Commonwealth Avenue to the river.

The Back Bay, as its name implies, was once a sodden region of salt marshes and mudflats. In 1814 the Massachusetts legislature chartered the Boston and Roxbury Mill Corporation to construct a long mill dam in the Charles River estuary that cut off the 450-acre tidal flats from the main channel of the river. Completed in 1821, the project proved to be less than a financial success, in part because of competition from mills using the more practical steam engine and because the efficiency of the water-driven mills was reduced when the Commonwealth permitted the construction of two railroad causeways across the bay which impeded the flow of water in the basin. By mid-century the project was manifestly a failure, and there was agitation on all sides to abandon milling operations and to fill the basin. One strong argument for filling was that the polluted bay constituted a serious health hazard. Boston had followed the practice of draining sewage into the harbor, counting on the ebbing tide to sweep the discharge out to sea. When the Back Bay was cut off from the cleansing flow of the tide, and the sewers continued to drain, the shallow bay became clogged with filth, which produced noxious odors. In 1849 the Health Department demanded the fill of the area in the interest of public health.

At about this time Boston's growth and commercial prosperity made investors hungry for new land to develop. There was already a tradition of filling in small bays and coves and the Back Bay appeared to be the largest area close at hand where it seemed possible to build a large residential community. The invention of the steam shovel and railroad was essential to the conversion of tidelands into solid ground. Gravel was brought from Needham, nine miles from Boston. One hundred and forty-five dirt cars, with eighty men, were employed night and day in loading and transporting the gravel. The trains consisted of thirty-five cars each; they made in the daytime sixteen trips and in the night nine or ten. Three trains were continually on the road during the day, and one arrived at the Back Bay every forty-five minutes. The train was filled by steam excavators that performed the work previously done by two hundred men. On an average, about 2500 cubic yards of fill was placed each day, approximately equal to 4500 superficial feet of land. The filling began at the east end of the bay in the autumn of 1857, and by 1900 the fill had gone beyond the present Kenmore Square area and the Fens.

The Back Bay was set out by Arthur Gilman in a street plan of oblong blocks in a formal gridiron pattern. On flat land a gridiron has few disadvantages and makes maximum use of the land. Like other towns developed in America at that time, planners hoped to keep a feeling of openness and overall low density by providing for squares and places for cultural and public buildings. Unfortunately, only two such squares were planned in the Back Bay; one was abandoned in order to get more house

lots to sell, and the other, Copley Square, has not managed to preserve its intended character.

Commonwealth Avenue was built 240 feet wide with a tree-lined park between its dual roadways. With its long vista, suggestive of the French boulevards being built at that time, Commonwealth Avenue stretched from the Public Garden on the east to the Fenway on the west. Individual deeds, involving the conveyance of property along the Avenue, included various covenants which imposed restrictions: that all houses be set back at least twenty feet from the property line; that all houses be built of masonry. Boston was one of the first American cities to establish some form of zoning regulations. In 1896 the Board of Park Commissioners established the height limit of seventy feet along Commonwealth Avenue and other city boulevards and parks. In 1898 height restrictions were increased to ninety feet upon all buildings along Copley Square. In 1903 the state legislature appointed a Commission on Height of Buildings in Boston to enact a general scheme of height restrictions and land use throughout the city. Boston was divided into two districts, one with limits of 125 feet and the other with limits of 80 feet. It was not until 1924 that the first zoning code embracing more than height controls was established for the city of Boston. This code remained in effect until the end of 1964. The present zoning code was adapted pursuant to an act of the Legislature which delegated power to the city to write, amend, and adopt its own zoning code. Under this enactment, the Zoning Commission is charged with the quasi-legislative responsibility of writing and amending the code, whereas the Board of Appeals is responsible for allowing variations from the requirements. Experience with the new code has proved that property owners are inclined to seek special relief through the Board of Appeals. The problem with this is that a comprehensive zoning plan drawn up by the Zoning Commission can be substantially varied by the Board of Appeals without full recognition of the effect of the day-to-day erosion of overall planning objectives.

The linear boulevard plan, coupled with the building restrictions, produced an architectural unity that set the Back Bay apart from earlier sections of Boston with their English-style streets and residential squares.

Strikingly different is the relationship of the individual house to the total environment. Houses in the South End were designed with less thought for the street as a complete concept. There, the street is lined by a succession of relentlessly independent house units, each with its own flight of front steps and its particular entrance porch. For a large part, the Back Bay has a more sophisticated unity. The individual house front counts for less than the block in which it is set.

Specific blocks were set aside for cultural and scientific institutions in the Back Bay. The Boston Public Library was granted land in Copley Square facing H. H. Richardson's magnificent Trinity Church and, after a decade of discussion and argument, engaged McKim, Mead & White to plan their classical building. The Harvard Medical School, Massachusetts Institute of Technology, and the Museum of Natural History (whose building now houses Bonwit Teller) moved into the Back Bay along with the Museum of Fine Arts to establish the area as the major intellectual center of "the Athens of America."

The peak of the Back Bay's desirability came at the turn of the nineteenth century. To the outsider, the district had an aura of opulence and social superiority; to the inhabitant, it was obvious that a neighborhood class system prevailed. It was generally considered that Beacon Street was occupied by people with family and money, Marlborough Street by those with family but no money, and Commonwealth Avenue the choice of those with money but no family. The water side of Beacon Street and the sunny side of Commonwealth Avenue were held to be the most prestigious of all. Henry James described what he saw: "It is all very rich and prosperous and monotonous . . . but, oh, so inexpressibly vacant! . . . speaking volumes for the possible serenity, the common decency, the quiet cohesion of a vast commercial and professional bourgeoisie left to itself."

Commonwealth Avenue was the critical connector in Frederick Law Olmsted's plan to make Boston's park system a continuous, unbroken chain of greenery. It stretched the mile and a half between the Public Garden and the Fenway, completing the link between Franklin Park and the Arnold Arboretum with the Public Garden and the Common. This grand scheme and its execution established this period as one of the most significant phases of the modern architectural movement—a movement led in Boston by Henry Hobson Richardson and by Olmsted. In 1885 *American Architecture and Building News* polled its readers on what they considered the most important buildings in the United States. H. H. Richardson's Trinity Church was first, followed by the U.S. Capitol, Hunt's Vanderbilt House, and Upjohn's Trinity Church in New York City. Fifth through tenth in importance were all buildings by Richardson, including Sever Hall at Harvard University and the Ames buildings in North Easton, Massachusetts.

In 1874 Charles Davenport created the Charles River Embankment in the same grand spirit, turning the outer edge of the one-time mudflats into a great public park. The trees had hardly grown before many of them were sacrificed in the name of progress to the automobile. The construction of Storrow Drive in 1937 reduced both the area and the accessibility of the park; and what was worse, it was only the first in a series of "improvements" on both sides of the river. "No one can understand the plight of the Back Bay today," observes Lewis Mumford, "and still prepare intelligently for its redevelopment, who does not understand the disintegrating effect of current transportation policies that conceive traffic as the only important function of urban life, to which every other urban need must be sacrificed. What the urban destruction inflicted by the railroad engineers only began, the highway engineers, who have added arrogance to the railroad engineers' ignorance, have carried through to a conclusion. Not the least damage done so far has been the virtual destruction of the Fenway park system."

334
348
482
414

Two trends, hardly noticeable until World War I, began to undermine the Back Bay's supremacy as the most fashionable residential district in Boston: the "rediscovery" and rehabilitation of the fine old houses of Beacon Hill and the beginning of the drift toward the suburbs made possible by the extension of public transit facilities and the advent of the automobile. As a result, during the 1920's Back Bay houses were partitioned into flats and converted to private schools, dormitories, or offices; and the construction of high-rise apartment buildings began. The new uses of the old buildings and their proximity to the growing universities provoked an influx of young people. Houses maintained as single-family dwellings were scarce by the 1940's. By 1950 the character of the Back Bay appeared irrevocably altered: a district planned for residential use had yielded to the demands of a changing population and a growing business community. The population of the Back Bay has grown since the mid-fifties, but the number of permanent residents has dropped steadily. Students living either in apartments, dormitories, or fraternity houses increased in number from 3000 in 1960 to 11,000 in 1967, out of a total district population of 21,500. A proposal for a new Back Bay campus as part of the Massachusetts Community College program drew cries of outrage because it would mean an increase in the already heavy student population of the area. Originally, there had been virtually no shops planned for the neighborhood, since tradesmen brought goods directly to their customers' homes, but they now exist in great numbers to supply the needs of the inhabitants. Many of these shops are squeezed tightly into old houses, in remodeled basements, or they announce themselves by replacing much of the main floor facade with a glass front.

The greatest visible change in the Back Bay has been the advent of the high-rise building. The condition of the subsoil (the famous Boston blue clay) has necessitated extensive pile and foundation work, the expense of

which could not be "justified" economically on a building holding the height allowed under the existing codes. Although buildings along the water side of Beacon Street have soared above the typical Back Bay buildings, nothing can compare with the disparity in scale between the Prudential Center complex, the new sixty-story John Hancock Tower, and their context. It is of ironic interest that the Hancock Tower is being erected on the site of the old Westminster Hotel, the upper story of which had to be removed because of its violation of the then existing height restrictions in Copley Square. However one views this particular mirror-glass enclosed tower of some two million square feet and its relationship, or lack of it, to Copley Square and Trinity Church, one has to assume that it will be the bellwether of all contemporary urban design problems.

Tunney Lee, former Chief Planner and Design Officer of the Boston Redevelopment Authority (B.R.A.), stated at a meeting at the Boston Architectural Center in 1968: "I am concerned about the prestige of the Back Bay, the vision and foresight of nineteenth-century architects and planners which we seem to have lost somewhere along the line. We seem to keep using up the patrimony that has been left to us, and we haven't really

built any new Copley Squares or Public Gardens. We seem to be using up our natural resources without putting any new ones in."

There are some positive sides to all this. While nineteenth-century planners tended to provide definitive boundaries to isolate an area such as the Back Bay from other parts of the city, twentieth-century planners see this community isolation as something that produces ghettos of one sort or another. It was felt in the last century that one of the reasons for the failure of the South End as a prime residential district was that the poor were allowed to live there as well as the rich. It is evident today that this kind of attitude does not lead to good neighborhoods. Both the Prudential Center and the John Hancock Tower complexes make extensive use of the air rights over the depressed rail lines and the Massachusetts Turnpike Extension, two traditional separators between the Back Bay and the South End. We are, in a way, building bridges across previous class and ethnic integrities, which we sometimes revere for their aesthetic value while forgetting the price paid in social rigidity.

Two of Boston's great chroniclers and critics see the Back Bay in different ways. In Walter Whitehill's view, "even though few of its houses are still occupied in the traditional manner, the Back Bay is still the handsomest and most consistent example of the American architecture of the second half of the nineteenth century now existing in the United States." And Lewis Mumford has written: "If the forbidding tidal marsh of the Back Bay could be drained and built over, there is no physical structure, whether solid as an expressway or as tall as an insurance building, that may not likewise be removed and replaced—once a better urban pattern and a more attractive mode of life have been conceived. That is the encouraging lesson the story of the Back Bay should teach us."

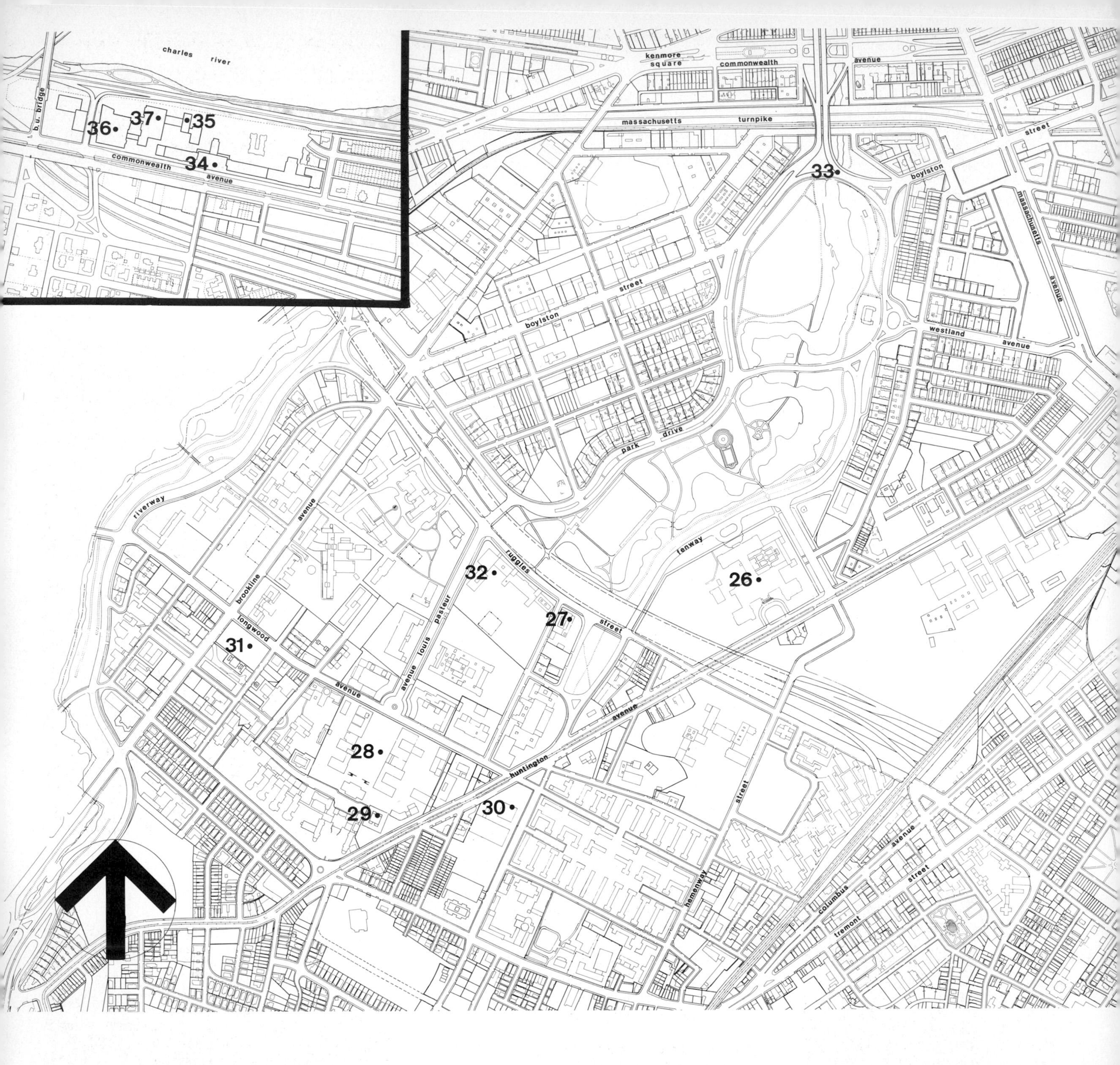

charles river
b.u. bridge
36
37
35
34
commonwealth
avenue
kenmore square
commonwealth
avenue
massachusetts turnpike
33
street
boylston
massachusetts avenue
boylston street
westland avenue
park drive
riverway
brookline avenue
ruggles
32
fenway
26
27
street
longwood
31
avenue
avenue louis pasteur
avenue
huntington
28
29
30
street
hemenway
columbus avenue
tremont street

The Fenway / Boston University

26. Museum of Fine Arts
Huntington Avenue and The Fenway
Guy Lowell; 1907–09
Additions: Hugh Stubbins and Associates; 1970–

27. Isabella Stewart Gardner Museum
280 The Fenway
Edward H. Sears; 1902

28. Harvard Medical School
Longwood Avenue
Shepley, Rutan & Coolidge; 1903–

29. Countway Library of Medicine
Harvard Medical School
Hugh Stubbins and Associates; 1965

30. Charlesbank Apartments
650 Huntington Avenue
Hugh Stubbins and Associates; 1963

31. Children's Hospital Medical Center Complex
Longwood Avenue
The Architects Collaborative
Master Planning, 1958–
Children's Inn, 1966–68

32. Simmons College
The Fenway
Campbell, Aldrich and Nulty
Library, 1961
Science Building, 1970–

33. Boylston Bridge
The Fenway
H. H. Richardson; 1880

34. Boston University
Charles River Campus
Commonwealth Avenue
Original Buildings: Cram and Ferguson; 1935–50

35. Boston University
Schools of Law and Education Building
Sert, Jackson and Gourley with Edwin T. Steffian; 1964

36. Boston University
George Sherman Union
Sert, Jackson and Gourley with Hoyle, Doran and Berry; 1963

37. Boston University
Mugar Library
Sert, Jackson and Associates with Hoyle, Doran and Berry; 1966

The Fenway

The citizens of Boston, finding themselves prosperous and in the midst of the 1869 land boom, began to agitate for a public park system. Petitions were signed, speeches were made and editorials were written—all demanding a Boston answer to New York's enviable Central Park.

Cries for a Park Commission went unheeded by the politicians for many years. In 1875, after the land and development boom had subsided, an act was passed creating such a commission, but leaving the purse strings in the hands of a reluctant City Council. Only in 1877, after concerted lobbying by speculators and renewed public pressure, did the City Council authorize the borrowing of funds necessary for the laying out of a park in an undeveloped part of the Back Bay: the Fens.

Plans were selected through an open competition, and Frederick Law Olmsted was retained as critic and consultant. Dissatisfied with what had been submitted, Olmsted made so many changes and revisions that the final plans, approved in 1878, were an expression of his own personal vision of a metropolitan greenery system. A particularly restricting condition had been set by the City Council: that land for the park could be purchased for no more than ten cents per square foot, a limitation which the opponents of the project succeeded in fastening upon the ordinance authorizing the park. They believed it would kill the whole scheme and save the city a great deal of money. Not only did it fail to thwart the park proposal, but it resulted in a cost for construction (to compensate for the poor land and odd configuration) that was without precedent in the history of park design. The price limitation resulted in producing a highly curious shape for the Fens—a shape that is virtually formless but somewhat resembles an amoeba with six projecting arms. Olmsted's plans managed to make the best of the irregular form and capitalize on the natural beauty of the area while turning it from an unsanitary, fetid swamp into a pleasant park.

As Commonwealth Avenue had been placed under the control of the Park Commission, it was included in the plans. Its long, sweeping curves were arranged to lead gracefully into the Fenway. Within the Fens itself the waterway was made to follow a crooked, winding path, simulating the natural course of a channel through a salt marsh. Whenever possible, Olmsted retained the existing features of the landscape, and he placed paths and bridges where they were least obtrusive.

The Fens is only one link in a chain of greenery often called "the Emerald Necklace."

This prototype for a series of open public spaces was conceived as a continuous band of parks and planted roadways. Olmsted constantly stressed the need for multiple facilities within one park. He wanted to satisfy all of the people, whether they liked to sit, stroll, play games or take a drive. He joined the Fenway to the already existing Public Garden and Commonwealth Avenue, extended it via the Riverway to Olmsted Park, the Arborway, and the Arnold Arboretum through Franklin Park which he designed in 1855, and beyond. This chain of parks linked by tree-lined roadways was more than a recreational complex; it provided a convenient and necessary transportational network for the vehicles of that time.

In the 1890's Charles Eliot, a Bostonian who had studied with Olmsted, extended the park system further, to the Blue Hills Reservation. When the Charles River was dammed, the planners followed Eliot's—and by implication, Olmsted's—example and built a linear park along the riverbanks.

The pressures of transportation and population have taken their toll on the Olmsted plans. His "Emerald Necklace" has been broken by highways, parking lots, overpasses and road widening. Links in the chain have been completely severed or at least partially obscured. The elevated highway that looms over the Charlesgate arm of the Fenway today has broken the spell of Olmsted's original romantic, naturalistic park of winding streams and twisting paths. H. H. Richardson's Boylston Street Bridge has been half obliterated to make room for the Massachusetts Turnpike. But Boston is still fortunate to retain some of the largest open green spaces in a central urban area—and it is not just their size, but their uniqueness as a part of the "country" in the midst of the city that mark them as evidence of Olmsted's singular vision and design.

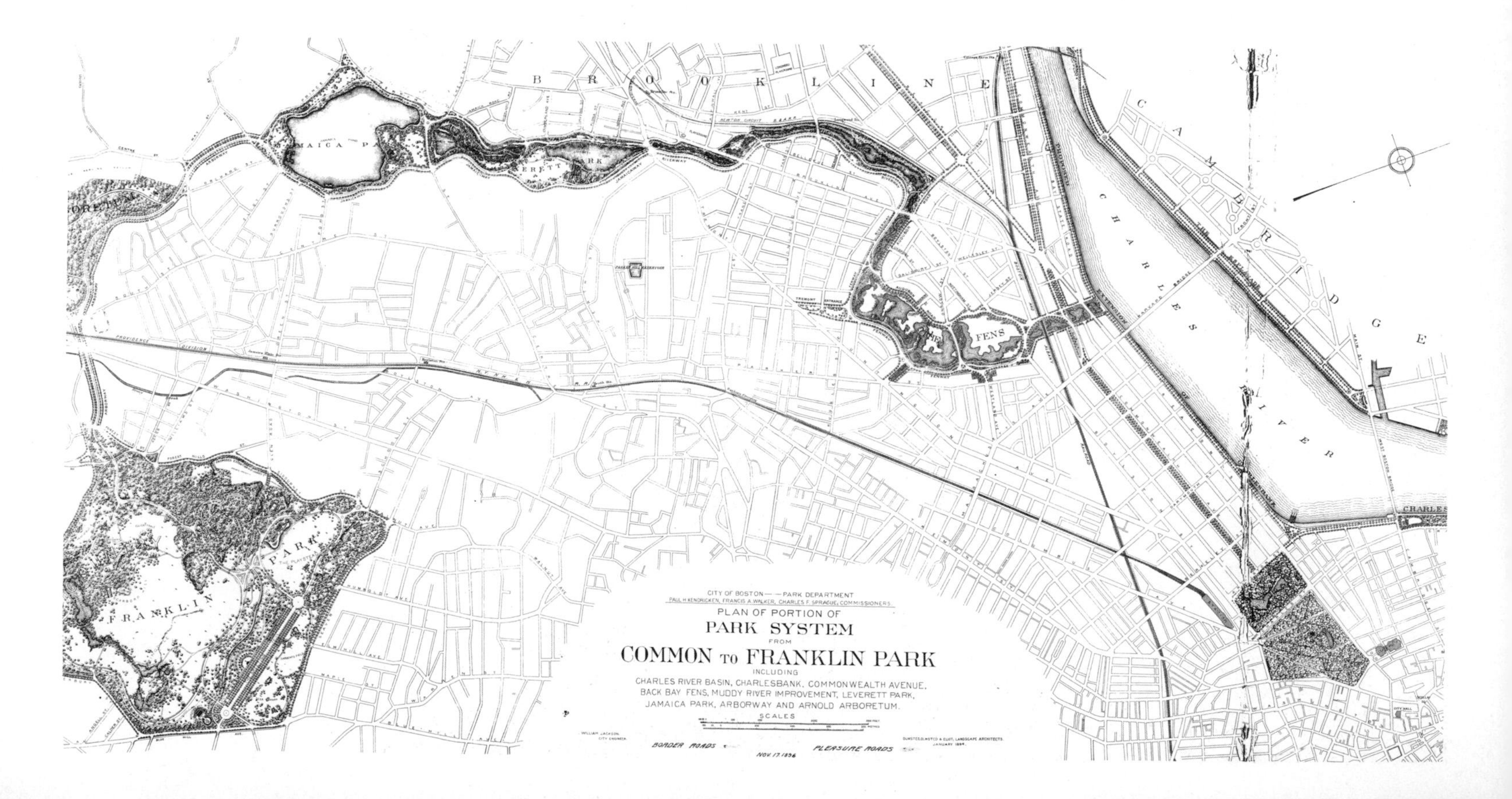

entral Business District /
Government Center
3

BOSTON CITY HALL

commercial street
fitzgerald
expressway
hanover
blossom street
merrimac street
chardon street
new sudbury street
new chardon
cambridge street
bowdoin street
n. market street
s. market street
state street
court street
congress street
new atlantic avenue
storrow drive
mount vernon street
chestnut street
beacon street
park street
milk street
washington street
franklin street
federal
fitzgerald avenue
atlantic avenue
expressway
charles street
tremont street
arlington street
berkeley street
clarendon street
boylston street
avenue
kneeland street
stuart
columbus
harrison avenue
summer street
new dorchester
street
1
2
3
4
5
6
7
8
9
10
11
12
13
14
15
16
17
18
19
20
21
22
23
24
25
26
27
28
29
30
31

Central Business District / Government Center

1. ▶ Boston Common
Oldest public park in America
1634 and 1824

2. ▶ King's Chapel
Tremont and School Streets
Peter Harrison; 1749–54

3. Old South Meeting House
Washington and Milk Streets
Joshua Blanchard; 1729

◀ **4.** Old State House
206 Washington Street
1712–13; Rebuilt: 1748
Alterations: Isaiah Rogers; 1830
Restored: George A. Clough; 1881–82

◀ **5.** Old City Hall
41–45 School Street
Gridley J. Fox Bryant and Arthur Gilman
1865

◀ **6.** Massachusetts Blue Cross-Blue Shield Headquarters Office Building
133 Federal Street
Anderson, Beckwith & Haible
with Paul Rudolph; 1961

7. First National Bank of Boston
100 Federal Street
Campbell, Aldrich & Nulty; 1971

8. ▶ Tremont-on-the-Common (apartments)
151 Tremont Street
S. J. Kessler & Sons; 1968

9. ▶ Government Center MBTA Station
City Hall Square
Exterior: Architects and Engineers for the Boston City Hall; 1968
Interior: Geometrics; 1969

◀ **10.** City Hall Square
Architects and Engineers for the
Boston City Hall
Stage one; 1969
Stage two (bridge to Dock Square); 1971

◀ **11.** New City Hall
City Hall Square
Architects and Engineers for the
Boston City Hall
(Kallmann, McKinnell and Knowles,
associated with Campbell, Aldrich and
Nulty, and Le Messurier & Associates); 1968

12. ▶ John F. Kennedy Federal Building
Government Center
The Architects Collaborative with
Samuel Glaser Associates; 1966

◀ **13.** Government Center Garage
Government Center
Samuel Glaser & Partners and
Kallman & McKinnell; 1970

14. National Shawmut Bank
67 Milk Street
The Architects Collaborative; 1971

◀ **15.** Health, Welfare and Education
Service Center for the Commonwealth
of Massachusetts
Government Center
Paul Rudolph, coordinating architect;
Shepley, Bulfinch, Richardson & Abbott
with Pedersen and Tilney, M. A. Dyer, and
Desmond and Lord
first half: 1970; second half: 1974

16. ▶ New England Merchants Bank Building
28 State Street
Edward L. Barnes and Emery Roth & Sons;
1969

17. ▶ Leverett Saltonstall Building
Government Center
Emery Roth & Sons; 1965

18. Bowdoin Street MBTA Station
6 Bowdoin Square
Sert, Jackson & Associates; 1968

19. ▶ Center Plaza (office building)
Government Center
Welton Beckett & Associates; 1966–69

20. Tufts-New England Medical Center
37 Bennett Street
The Architects Collaborative and
Tufts-New England Medical Center
Planning Office; long range

21. Boston Five Cent Savings Bank
24 School Street
Kallmann & McKinnell; 1971

22. ▶ Sears Crescent Building (rehabilitation)
City Hall Square
Stull Associates; 1969

23. ▶ Old Corner Bookstore
Washington and School Streets
Thomas Crease; 1711

24. One Beacon Street (office building)
Employers-Commercial Union Companies
Skidmore, Owings & Merrill; 1972

◀ **25.** Old West Church
Cambridge and Lynde Streets
Asher Benjamin; 1806

26. ▶ First Harrison Grey Otis House
Headquarters of the Society for the
Preservation of New England Antiquities
141 Cambridge Street
Charles Bulfinch; 1796–97

◀ **27.** State Street Bank Building
225 Franklin Street
Pearl Street Associates (F. A. Stahl
& Associates, Hugh Stubbins & Associates,
Le Messurier & Associates); 1966

28. Federal Reserve Bank
Atlantic Avenue and Summer Street
Hugh Stubbins & Associates; 197–

29. New England Trade and
Transportation Center
Massachusetts Port Authority
South Station Complex
Sert, Jackson and Associates; 197–

◀ **30.** Boston Company Building
1 Boston Place
Pietro Belluschi and Emery Roth & Sons
1970

31. Keystone Building
High and Congress Streets
Pietro Belluschi and Emery Roth & Sons;
1970

Central Business District / Government Center

Downtown Boston has been called at once the most charming, most dilapidated, most delightful, and most frustrating collection of urban real estate in all of the United States.

The cow has often been made a scapegoat for the confusing street patterns of downtown Boston, but the circuitous roads and narrow alleys of the city are explained by more than the meanderings of cattle to pasture on the Common. Boston was dotted with hills, surrounded by marshes, coves, and creeks, and isolated on a peninsula in its earliest days. Street patterns evolved as the first Bostonians circumnavigated natural obstacles, filled in land to connect their community to other regions, or expanded into the harbor to enlarge the waterfront's wharfing and warehousing capacity.

By 1835 the Central Business District had become divided into areas by trade. The State Street section housed banks; the Faneuil Hall region served as a marketplace; upper Washington Street dealt in dry goods; land to the south and east abounded in warehouses and wholesale businesses. These distinctions have grown hazier and more inclusive as the years have passed, but to a large extent are as true today as they were in the 1880's; the only major change has been the drift of commercialism down Boylston and Newbury Streets and the new commercial core at the Prudential Center.

In 1844 R. F. Gourlay, whose imaginative plans for the Back Bay were to cause a sensation in the 1850's, wrote prophetically: "Already Washington Street is crowded to excess; and, every day, we witness inconvenience from the noise and collision of carriages. What would it be if there were a million of residents and tens of thousands of visitors?" Traffic congestion on the narrow, winding streets grew worse, and by 1890 studies for a subway system were begun. The first portion of the subway, from Park Street to the Public Garden, was opened in 1898 and cost the city $4,350,000. The subway stop at Washington Street was first used in 1908, and its benefit to the downtown area was witnessed by the enormous passenger flow at Park and Washington stations. The Central Business District, now more easily accessible, was fully formed: sixty percent of the region was man-made, recovered from marshes and the sea or acquired by leveling off the hills.

The automobile wreaked havoc on downtown Boston. The unplanned streets, having evolved organically according to topography and early usage, could not accommodate the incredible stream of traffic that snarled each day through the area. Boston had been a pedestrian city; the patterns of movement it could cope with were those of people on foot. Narrow, twisting alleys presented problems even in the nineteenth century. Things were difficult enough in the days of horse and buggy transportation, and when automobiles became common in Boston, chaos broke loose. Vehicular circulation became hopelessly clogged; parking problems seemed unanswerable.

Until the 1950's building in downtown Boston stagnated. Washington economist Robert Gladstone reported to the Boston Redevelopment Authority, "The potential is outstanding; only 25% of the existing space is really first class—and that first class space is about 100% occupied." The first of the new buildings was the 30-story, $30 million State Street Bank Building constructed in 1965 and containing some 800,000 square feet of office space. There is question as to whether it was the commercial success of this venture that led others to erect new office buildings in the Central Business District or if it was the fact that suddenly one bank had displayed its name on top of a new building that could be seen from almost any spot in Boston. After that came the New England Merchants Bank, the Boston Company Building, the First National Bank of Boston, and on and on. A similar trend is seen in the John Hancock Company's plan for a major building on Copley Square that happens to be just slightly taller than the Prudential Center Tower several blocks away.

The great conglomerate of styles in the Central Business District speaks clearly of the earlier random development. The sites of the new buildings appear to be as much affected by the eighteenth-century topographical features—most of which are no longer recognizable in themselves—as any new urban plan.

At one time, Development Administrator Edward J. Logue brought in Victor Gruen to provide a plan for the area. Gruen's plans, published in 1967, called for seven nuclei of activity, each connected to the next by a vast mall located on Washington Street between Boylston and State Streets. This, in turn, would be crossed by another mall running from Tremont Street to South Station. The idea was to tie the weaker elements of downtown Boston into the stronger ones. But both the B.R.A. and the Central Business District businessmen objected to the length of the mall as well as the widening of Tremont Street. The success or failure of any mall

Albert's
HOSIERY
TOW AREA

Snack Bar

ATE STREET BANK
CITY of BOSTON PARKING FACILITY
PARKING
ALL DAY
AIR
PARK HERE

scheme depends upon the success or failure of the downtown traffic plan. The major parking facility at the proposed New England Trade and Transportation Center at the present South Station is suspended in bureaucratic inertia, and although other smaller parking structures are being built, the overall traffic pattern feeding the area is still hopelessly snarled.

The B.R.A. did some planning of its own, and when considered with Gruen's suggestions, yielded several interesting proposals: a cultural and entertainment center at lower Washington Street and the creation of new office space combined with a strengthening of existing properties on upper Washington Street. If these plans work, "new Boston's" downtown will be easier to get into by transit or car, to move around in, and to park in. If, at the same time, it is possible to preserve the qualities that give the area its special flavor, then the plan will have succeeded in doing that rare thing—bringing together historic buildings and traditional scale with the economic needs of the "new Boston."

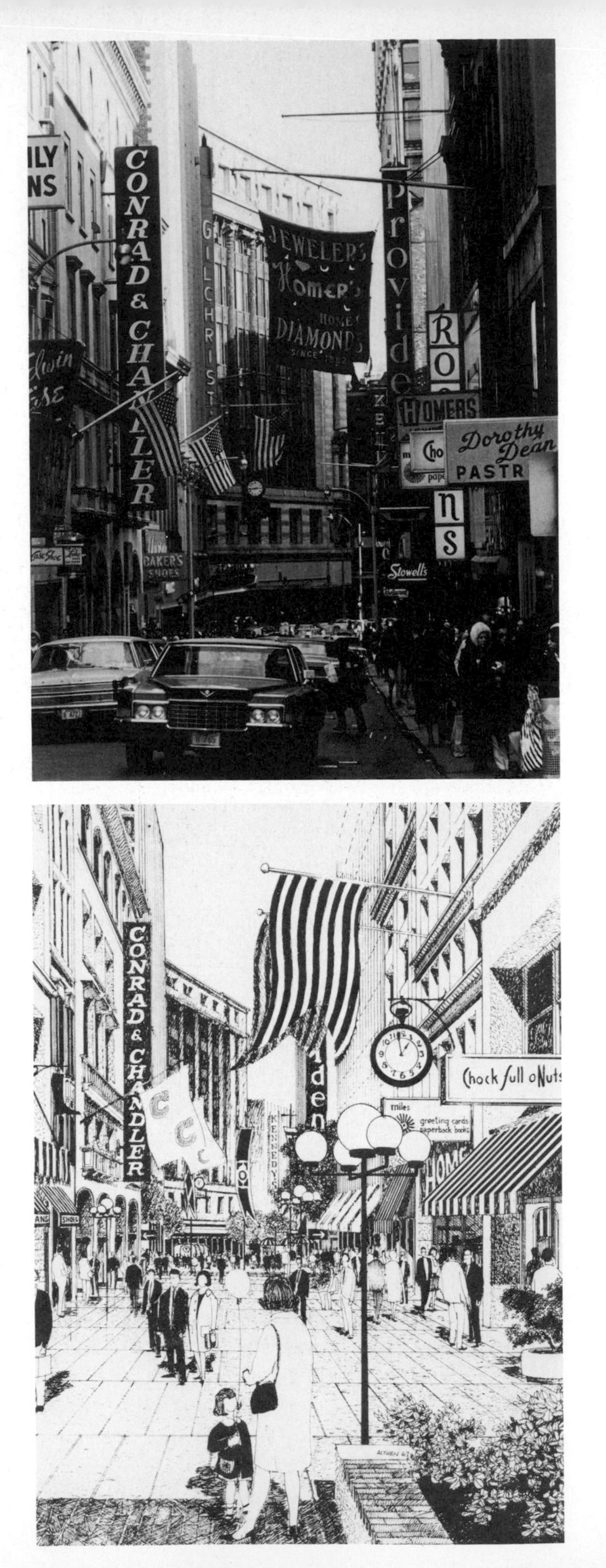

One of the edges of the Central Business District is formed by the Boston Common and the Public Garden. That the Common belongs to the people rather than to the city is important. None of the land of the Common—now the oldest public park in America—can be sold, no building can be constructed on it, and no roads may run through it without the express consent of the citizens. Although it began as a common cow pasture and militia training ground, it was and still is the scene of festivals and political rallies. It was the rallying ground of patriots during the earliest days of the Revolution and was recently the setting for a Vietnam Peace Action demonstration that drew well over a hundred thousand people. It has become the American counterpart of Hyde Park Speakers' Corner in London and is still the one place in Boston that generates a true feeling of public ownership. In *The Book of Boston* (1917) Robert Shackleton wrote: ". . . the people of Boston will retain

their liberty so long as they retain their Common, and will sink into commonplaceness only if they give up their Common. It is, in a double sense, a Common heritage."

The position of the Common, between the Central Business District and Beacon Hill, has made it a convenient and attractive meeting ground for groups of all kinds and a haven for office workers seeking a quiet stroll during lunch hour. It is here that there begins to be evidence of the changing life in Boston. While the Beacon Hill side maintains its serene Bulfinch dignity and human scale, the first intrusions of the new scale have shown themselves along the downtown side. The high-rise apartment building on Tremont Street appears to be only the first of a group of such towers that will fringe the Common.

The Public Garden was annexed to the Common in 1824 at the suggestion of Mayor Quincy. The Public Garden is formally laid out into gardens, paths, and ponds. The Common is wilder, more natural, and gives a feeling of the open country. At the end of the nineteenth century Frederick Law Olmsted made his great plan to link the Common and Public Garden with all of the city's green spaces. This continuous drive passed down Commonwealth Avenue to the Fenway and linked Roxbury's Franklin Park and the Arnold Arboretum to the rest. The Common and Public Garden together are probably the largest open space in a downtown area in the United States. In a congested, constantly expanding city this can be not so much a luxury as a necessity.

The other edge of the Central Business District is formed by the new Government Center. The crowded, narrow streets of downtown Boston almost burst into broad boulevards at the sixty-acre Center with the

new City Hall acting as a fulcrum to the twenty-six-story John F. Kennedy federal office building, the twenty-two-story Saltonstall state office building, the immense State Service Center for Health, Welfare, and Education, the long, curved Center Plaza office building, and the smaller government buildings as well as the cluster of bank towers being built around the edges.

The Government Center was built on what was once Scollay Square, Boston's honky-tonk district, decrepit and shabby. But it was centrally located and easily reached by three subway lines at five stations. Added to this, its proximity to the State House and old City Hall made the site a natural selection.
By the mid-1950's, the general inconvenience of having the various offices and departments of the several branches of the government widely scattered all over town put additional pressure on making a move to centralize. In 1959 planners Adams, Howard, and Greeley released a study which was favorably received, and hopes began to rise that it might help in the rejuvenation of the downtown area. With the election of Mayor John F. Collins and his Development Administrator Edward J. Logue, plans were started on the Government Center. I. M. Pei was called in to plan the location and size of the buildings and to transform the existing street pattern into a workable means of circulation in and around the new Center. He reduced the twenty-two existing streets into four north–south routes and two east–west arcs. Working closely with Walter Whitehill, Pei chose to retain certain historic buildings and those with a tradition of special usage—such as the 1841 Sears Crescent, which had been a bookselling center for more than a

century, as well as a well-trod pathway to Faneuil Hall. Pei's contribution went still further; he established the City Hall as the keystone of the entire project and in an "envelope plan" set the heights and sizes of the other buildings. In one case he proposed a new office building on a site bordering the area which was then occupied by two serviceable buildings. Besides offering evidence for economic viability both to developers and the city tax department, he pointed out that the new building would provide a natural terminus for Washington Street and that its plaza would be both a spacious setting for the Old State House and a link between it and the new Government Center.

Boston then held a national design competition for the City Hall. From some 250 entries, eight finalists were chosen; and from these, a team of young and relatively unknown architects was selected: Kallmann, McKinnell & Knowles. "Often in the past," writes Walter Whitehill, "a winning design in competition has been laid aside unused. This one was promptly executed. The building is logically planned, with departments receiving many visitors in the great base, which the architects call 'the Mound'; ceremonial space—mayor's office and council chamber—above; and pure bureaucracy, not requiring much public access, tucked away on the three top floors. The City Hall is low and huge, with Mycenaean or Aztec overtones in its massiveness. In my view, it is as fine a building for its time and place as Boston has ever produced. Traditionalists who long for a revival of Bulfinch simply do not realize that one does not achieve a handsome monster either by enlarging, or endlessly multiplying, the attractive elements of smaller structures."

MTA
RAPID TRANSIT
TRAINS
CONNECTIONS
ALL POINTS
G.C.C.
UNIFORM CO.
UNIFORMS
MADE TO
MEASURE
SONS of LIBERTY 1766
1776
DENTISTS
LIBERTY
CENTER
...you can be
there's none

T

N - MASS. PIKE
TOWN
ESSEX

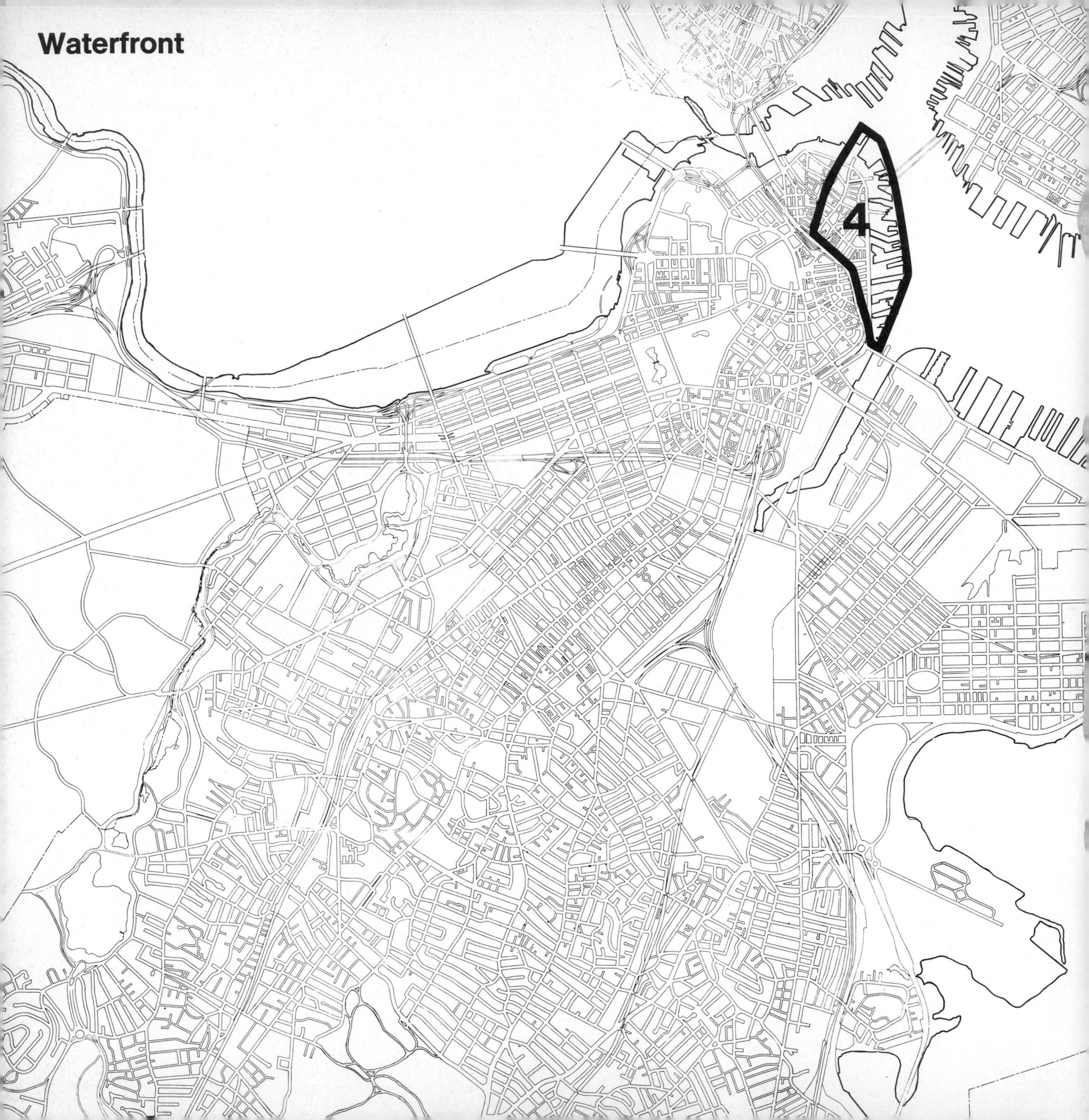
Waterfront
4

commercial street
fitzgerald
expressway
blossom street
merrimac street
street
chardon
new
new sudbury street
cambridge street
bowdoin street
hanover
street
n. market street
s. market street
court street
state street
street
mount vernon street
chestnut street
beacon street
storrow drive
milk street
congress street
franklin street
street
street
washington
tremont street
park street
charles street
arlington street
berkeley street
clarendon
street
boylston street
avenue
street
kneeland street
stuart
columbus
harrison avenue
federal street
fitzgerald avenue
atlantic avenue
summer street
new atlantic avenue
expressway
street
new dorchester
street
1
2
3
4
5
6
7
8
9
10
11
12
13
14
15
16
17
18
19

Waterfront

◀ **1.** Faneuil Hall
Dock Square
John Smibert; 1740–42
Reconstruction; 1762–63
Enlargement: Charles Bulfinch; 1805–06

2. ▶ Quincy Market and
North & South Market Street Buildings
Alexander Parris; 1824–26

◀ **3.** St. Stephen's Church
(originally New North Church)
401 Hanover Street
Charles Bulfinch; 1804

4. ▶ Commercial Wharf Warehouses
Off 80 Atlantic Avenue
1826
Renovation into apartments; 1954–68

◀ **5.** Prince Building (conversion to apartments)
63 Atlantic Avenue
J. Timothy Anderson & Associates; 1966–69

6. Commercial Block Building
128–142 Commercial Street
Gridley J. Fox Bryant; 1856

7. ▶ New England Aquarium
Central Wharf
Cambridge Seven Associates; 1969

8. ▶ Old North Church (Christ Church Episcopal)
193 Salem Street
William Price (Printseller); 1723

9. Paul Revere Mall
Hanover Street
Planned by the City of Boston; 1933

10. Blackstone Block
Congress Street behind City Hall

◀ **11.** Cast Iron Building
(now McLauthlin Elevator Company)
120 Fulton Street
Possibly Daniel Badger; c. 1850

◀ **12.** Lewis Wharf Granite Buildings
Renovation (first phase): Carl Koch and Associates; 1971–

13. ▶ Mercantile Wharf Building
75–117 Commercial Street
Gridley J. Fox Bryant; 1857

◀ **14.** Paul Revere House
Old North Square
c. 1677

15. Harbor Towers (apartments)
India and Rowes Wharves, Atlantic Avenue
I. M. Pei & Partners; 197–

16. ▶ Grain and Flour Exchange Building
(originally Chamber of Commerce Building)
177 Milk Street
Shepley, Rutan & Coolidge; 1890–92

◀ **17.** Custom House
State Street & India Wharf
Ammi B. Young; 1837–47
▶ Tower: Peabody and Stearns; 1913–15

18. Hancock House
Oldest extant brick building in Boston
Marshall Street
c. 1680

19. Moses Pierce-Hichborn House
Old North Square
c. 1711

Waterfront

Boston's waterfront, for long a bleak, desolate expanse, is just beginning to show signs of a vigorous new life. The area marked for renewal takes in a mile of wharves and about sixty-five acres to the west of Atlantic Avenue, extending almost to the steps of the new City Hall. It is a part of the city characterized by half-vacant buildings, broken windows, empty sites where buildings have been recently torn down, and evidence of vandalism and fire almost anywhere you choose to look. This area also contains some of the most cherished historic land in the city, including such structures as Long Wharf (from which the British troops were evacuated in 1776), Faneuil Hall, and Quincy Market.

The waterfront has been changing its shape for more than three hundred years. Originally it was a common landing ground with ferries to the few neighboring communities. Individuals living along the waterfront were granted the use of adjacent land for wharfing and loading vessels. Suppliers of maritime fittings and provisions settled among shipbuilders and sailors and enjoyed a flourishing trade. "From the early years of the settlement," writes Walter Whitehill, "merchant owners of waterfront property were constantly building wharves into the harbor, and thus began the inexorable encroachment of land upon water that has marked the history of Boston."

Construction of wharves was not always a simple matter because much of the land skirting the waterfront was a mass of marshes, creeks, and coves; firm foundations were achieved only through considerable effort. In the 1640's grants were made to individuals who undertook the conversion of swampy wastelands into profitable wharves. The earliest grant of this sort was made to Valentine Hill, who created a successful Town Cove in the area that is now Faneuil Hall Square. The town dock divided Boston into North and South Ends; the orderly wharves built by Hill fronted the south side, and the north cove was left untouched. Shipping trade and related maritime industries prospered, and the waterfront was the most vital, thickly settled part of town. This included the North End, which became the home of sea captains, sailors, merchants, and shipbuilders, who chose to live where they could keep an eye on their property and an ear out for news of the latest promising enterprise. A South Battery was built in 1666, and wharves and warehouses proliferated.

In 1673 the most ambitious attempt to secure the safety of the harbor was made in the construction of the Barricado, a wharf twenty feet wide and 2200 feet long. This fortification stretched from the East Cove to the foot of Copp's Hill. As the years passed without enemy attack, and because it served no commercial function, the wall was neglected and allowed to crumble. Its fragments remained long past the heyday of the shipping era. The Barricado had been built at the expense of private citizens who, in return, had the right to build wharves and warehouses between the wall and the shore. The legal question of who has title to that area lying under water only at high tide had to be resolved before private owners would undertake new development. The unsettled question of possession was one reason why they allowed their present properties to deteriorate.

The building of Long Wharf at the foot of King (now State) Street in 1710 was also undertaken as a private venture, by Captain Oliver Noyes and his associates. This amounted to extending King Street through the Cove, across the Barricado, and well into the harbor. Long Wharf was lined with continuous shops and warehouses and permitted the direct loading and unloading of the largest ships of the time without the use of boats or lighters. King Street became the broad avenue from the heart of Boston to "that part of the world that really counted."

The first half of the eighteenth century was a happy, boisterous, prosperous time for the waterfront area. In 1722 the town had 12,000 people and more than forty wharves and twelve shipyards; it was acclaimed as the largest town in British North America. Thriving on its maritime industries, Boston enjoyed a successful share of the "Triangular Trade" with Britain and the West Indies. George Weston, Jr. wrote in *Boston Ways—High, By and Folk* (1957): "The nostalgic Water Front seems to sit and dream of a past magnificence, when—in a single year, 1748—540 vessels cleared from and 430 entered, the port of Boston, not counting coastal or fishing vessels. In a single day of that year, seventy ships sailed from Boston for ports throughout the world."

In 1657 a Town House had been built; it became Boston's first Exchange, the true center of the business life of the city and, indeed, of the whole of New England. The merchants of Boston congregated there while, in chambers above, the monthly courts were held. The Town House, provided by the legacy of Robert Keayne, a merchant tailor, remained the core of commercial activity for almost a hundred years. In 1742 Peter Faneuil gave Boston its famous market and assembly hall, designed by John Smibert. Destroyed by fire in 1761, the building was reconstructed with funds raised in a public lottery. In 1805 Charles Bulfinch enlarged it and added a third story to the brick landmark. Its ground floor has always been used as a market—the donor's original wish—and within its halls much of Boston's political history was made. The area around this market and meeting place had been built up in the seventeenth century, but neglect over the years had let it degenerate into more of a rubbish heap than a wharf. Mayor Quincy had the town dock area filled and the wharves between it and the Long Wharf built over; in the newly created open space he had built a two-story granite market building 555 feet long, designed by Alexander Parris, which was flanked on either side by the recently laid out North and South Market Streets.

Quincy Market and Faneuil Hall have deteriorated badly during the twentieth century, and only through a federal grant has a study for their restoration been made possible. Plans include the removal of the long-established markets, and the study must investigate possible alternative uses for these historically significant buildings. Since no one wants to see them turn into a Bostonian Williamsburg, the new use must be relevant to the buildings and yet have an active life of its own. This has been accomplished successfully at Sears Crescent, and it is hoped that it can be done equally well at the "old" City Hall, which is being sold by the city to private developers.

In 1817 Shubael Bell wrote the following description of India and Central Wharves: "The completion of this undertaking, unparalleled in commercial History, is a proof of the enterprise, the wealth, and the persevering Industry of Bostonians. The number of stores are fifty four, and the length of the tier nearly thirteen hundred feet, of four stories. The wharf itself is considerably longer, and about one hundred and fifty feet in breadth, inclosed by a strong stone wall. The buildings are supported on piles and have water proof cellars. The wharf is already lined with vessels and crowded with business." (Quoted by Walter Whitehill in *Boston—A Topographical History,* 2nd ed., pp. 86–88.)

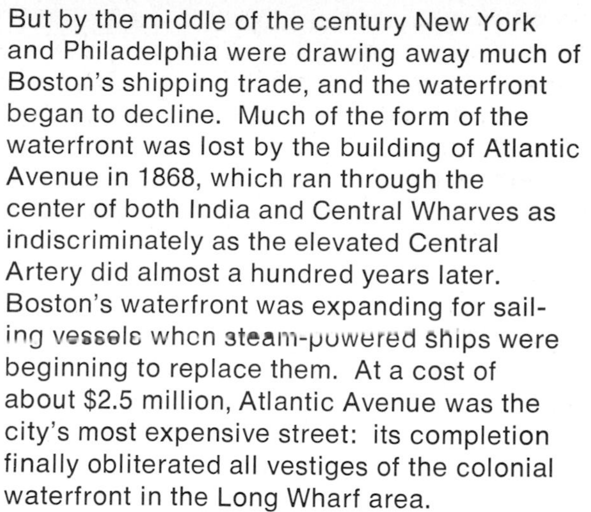

But by the middle of the century New York and Philadelphia were drawing away much of Boston's shipping trade, and the waterfront began to decline. Much of the form of the waterfront was lost by the building of Atlantic Avenue in 1868, which ran through the center of both India and Central Wharves as indiscriminately as the elevated Central Artery did almost a hundred years later. Boston's waterfront was expanding for sailing vessels when steam-powered ships were beginning to replace them. At a cost of about $2.5 million, Atlantic Avenue was the city's most expensive street: its completion finally obliterated all vestiges of the colonial waterfront in the Long Wharf area.

The wharves along Atlantic Avenue were used by fishermen and fish dealers until the opening of Fish Pier in South Boston in 1914, which caused a migration of major proportions. The wharves were deserted; what had been Boston's major industry sought other shores. "But fine views of the harbor," comments Walter Whitehill, "combined with low rents, led various venturesome Bostonians to create a *vie de bohème* in the ramshackle buildings of T Wharf and in the nobler warehouses of Long, Commercial, and Lewis Wharves."

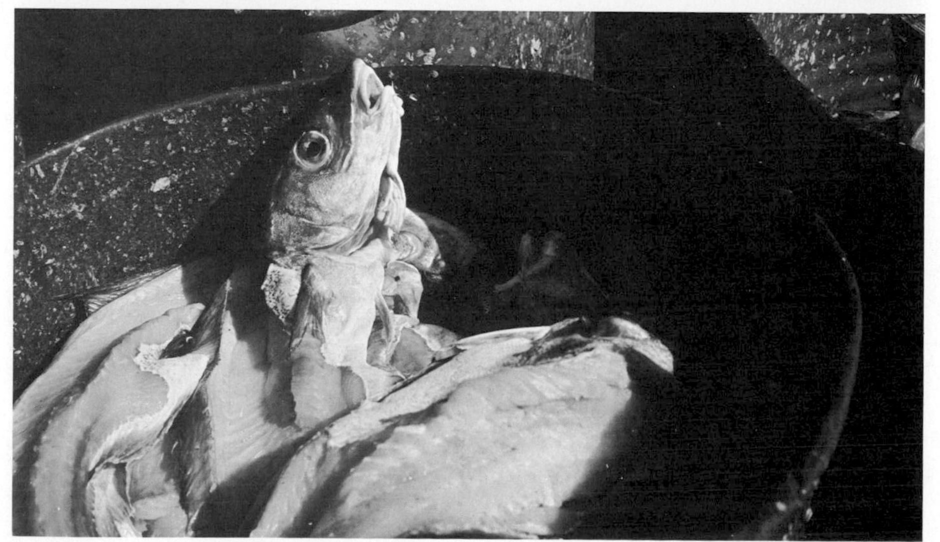

By 1962 the Waterfront Redevelopment Division had made a study of the problem and was ready to release its plan: office and general business buildings and residential towers were located near the Central Business District; middle-income housing bordered the North End; use was made of the wharves for new and rehabilitated apartments as well as other commercial and recreational attractions such as the Aquarium, motels, marinas, and public open spaces. Of prime importance was that broad, littoral road, Atlantic Avenue, which was to be bent inland to create a large, developable parcel on the water side, uncut by a major road. The planners went out of their way to preserve all historic buildings so that there

COLD STORAGE

would be a sense of continuity between past and future. In spite of the six-lane, elevated highway called the Central Artery, which cut through the area like a Chinese wall, the plan called for an attempt to rebuild the pedestrian connection between the waterfront and the Faneuil Hall-Quincy Market district.

The beginning of the implementation has been tentative at best. The warehouse owned by the Prince Spaghetti Company was saved from its intended demolition and renovated into luxury apartments overlooking the water. Commercial Wharf has been slowly remodeled into shops, offices, and apartments; the Aquarium on Central Wharf has been completed and is proving to be a great attraction for visitors. The first of the Harbor Towers on Rowes and India Wharves are under construction. Much of the area still lies fallow, and it will take a determined effort on the part of the city to keep developers interested, in spite of the fact that the waterfront is perhaps one of Boston's greatest unused assets.

The waterfront is only the edge of the harbor; the past half century has seen the same deterioration and decay in and on the water as has occurred along the mainland. The harbor is polluted and littered with debris. The islands lying off the coast of Boston are potentially both the most spacious recreational land in the region and the one closest to the most densely populated areas. So far, however, no effective plan has been prepared for the development of the harbor and its islands.

South End

beacon
street
marlborough
street
commonwealth
avenue
newbury
street
boylston
street
dartmouth
street
clarendon
street
berkeley
street
arlington
street
charles
street
tremont
street
massachusetts
turnpike
herald
street
massachusetts
avenue
huntington
avenue
dover
street
avenue
warren
avenue
union
park
columbus
rutland
square
west
canton
street
east
brookline
street
tremont
street
chester
square
shawmut
avenue
washington
worcester
square
harrison
avenue
street
albany
forsyth
street
1
2
3
4
5
6
7
8
9
10
11
12
13
14

South End

1. ▶ Castle Square (housing)
492 Tremont Street (management)
Samuel Glaser & Partners; 1967

2. ▶ Neighborhood-built Playground
Canton Street and Shawmut Avenue
1969

3. ▶ Worcester Square
1051

4. Boston University School of Medicine
Basic Sciences Instructional Building; 1969
80 East Concord Street
Housman Research Building; 1968
732 Harrison Avenue
Shepley, Bulfinch, Richardson & Abbott

◀ 5. Infill Housing Prototype
19–21 East Springfield Street
Stull Associates; 1969

◀ 6. Chester Square
Massachusetts Avenue between Tremont
Street and Shawmut Avenue
1850

7. Neighborhood-built Playground
Massachusetts and Columbus Avenues
1968

8. Northeastern University
360 Huntington Avenue
Shepley, Bulfinch, Richardson & Abbott;
1936–70
(about 15 buildings completed at this time)

◀ 9. Old Flower Market
(originally built to house the
Cyclorama commemorating the Civil War;
1884) Conversion to Flower Market; 1923
539 Tremont Street

10. Tremont Homes
Tremont Street from Rutland Square
to Worcester Square
Sert, Jackson & Associates; 1971

11. ▶ Union Park
1851

12. Goodwill Industries Rehabilitation Center
Arlington Street and Columbus Avenue
Perry, Dean and Stewart; 1971

13. Animal Rescue League
10 Chandler Street
Hugh Stubbins & Associates; 1956

South End

The South End is the no-man's land through which Bostonians pass when traveling between the Roxbury–Dorchester area and downtown. Much of the traffic that rumbles through its streets has nothing to do with the district, nor do many of the people on its sidewalks have either a home or business in the neighborhood. To many, South End and Skid Row are synonymous. The South End has the largest "rooming house" population in Boston and one of the lowest "school completion" records. In a 1967 Diagnostic Report prepared by the Boston Redevelopment Authority on the South End Renewal Area, only 5 percent of the people reported owning their own homes, and although 25 percent had completed high school, less than 5 percent held a college degree. Since the early 1960's, however, a new group has been moving into the South End. These people, to a large extent, are young professionals who recognize both the quality of the houses and the proximity to the city center as factors in making a successful urban life—and at a cost they could not find anywhere else in Boston. They have quietly rehabilitated fine old houses from a hodgepodge of run-down rooms and apartments, and have settled in around the small parks and narrow streets with a renewed sense of community pride.

The history of the city in the eighteenth century provides evidence as to why these fine houses were built in the South End. Boston, in those days, was almost an island, connected to the mainland by a thin strand of land often submerged by high tides. After the Revolution a sea wall was built along this connecting road to Roxbury to protect it and the few houses scattered along the neck. At the beginning of the nineteenth century the city began to fill in around the neck lands and sell these reclaimed areas. In 1833 a South Cove Corporation was chartered to continue filling in an additional seventy acres, and other contracts for filling and development were made by the Commonwealth during succeeding years.

Many of the old neighborhoods are rich in history but impoverished by decay. The population of the South End declined from 55,400 in 1950 to 24,900 in 1965; during the same period over 50 percent of the buildings were judged to be substandard. Still there was strong resentment against large-scale renewal. In the early days of Boston's renewal program, the West End, the declining Italian neighborhood at the foot of Beacon Hill, was the first big target. All the old buildings were bulldozed to make way for a group of undistinguished high-rise, high-rent apartments. Many charged that what renewal really meant was poor man's removal.

The bulldozer had cleared over forty-four acres in the West End to make room for 2400 new apartment units, and the people of the South End did not want that to happen in their community. There was a strong desire both to maintain the scale and character of the district as well as to insure that the buildings meant to replace the run-down tenements would be for the people who were being displaced. The poorer classes had taken over the South End when it was abandoned by the rich, and they determined now to stay in the neighborhood they had created. There was no doubt that new housing in vast quantity was needed, but no one wanted to be moved out to make room for it, as had happened in other renewal areas. In the early 1950's the Boston Housing Authority had built the Cathedral Project, a bleak group of high-rise yellow brick buildings typical of that period—a mass of some 500 apartment units neatly isolated from the rest of the community by scale and boundary—very clearly reading as Public Housing. In the late 1960's private developers, under one of the programs of the National Housing Act, built the Castle Square project. This also comprised about 500 apartments, but in spite of economic realities which were to determine heights and densities, there was an attempt to connect this area with the rest of the community through the use of materials, color, and scale.

The Puerto Rican residents of the South End have gained what many groups in the city have been denied—a voice in planning the redevelopment of their neighborhood. The Emergency Tenants' Council, representing 1500 residents, has been developing plans for "Parcel 19" in an attempt to maintain the integrity of the Spanish-speaking community. One of the main differences between their plan and that proposed by the B.R.A. was that the E.T.C. wanted to close off most of the streets in the area to produce a pedestrian community; the B.R.A. recognized the basic character of the existing neighborhood and wanted to maintain the "block" structure that is so characteristic of the South End.

Another group, the South End Tenants' Council, has formed a management firm to rehabilitate, maintain, and manage thirty-four buildings. This is one of the first times in the country that the ownership of the buildings undergoing renewal has been in the hands of the people who will occupy those buildings. Programs of self-help, training, and rehabilitation have been undertaken to insure as much community control as possible. Groups have cooperated and turned vacant lots into neighborhood playgrounds with the very minimal amount of outside financing necessary. All this has not come about easily. Different groups, representing different factions, have fought each other as well as the proverbial City Hall for control, money has been tight, and training of unskilled labor slow. But this may still prove to be one of the outstanding rehabilitation projects undertaken in the city.

Development of the South End came slowly, and settlement was further hampered by what was considered its "remoteness" from the city proper. As late as 1854 Boston's mayor complained that there was nothing there but a wide waste of neglected territory. What finally helped establish a fashionable occupancy of the South End was the construction in 1856 of a horse-railroad which connected the district to the city center.

Following this, there was a pronounced movement of upper-class families to the neighborhood. Union Park, Chester Park, Worcester and Rutland Squares became particularly favorite locations. Most of these squares were built cooperatively by the persons who owned abutting property, and their upkeep was a private concern. Walter Whitehill describes the South End thus: "Beginning with the fifties it rapidly grew into a region of symmetrical blocks of high-shouldered, comfortable red brick or brownstone houses, bow-fronted and high-stooped, with mansard roofs, ranged along spacious avenues, intersected by cross streets that occasionally widened into tree-shaded squares and parks, whose central gardens were enclosed by neat cast iron fences."

Like many great expectations, the success of the South End did not live up to prophesy. Although the area was respectable and full of citizens of substantial wealth, the price of land had been set at an inordinately high rate to insure a uniformly upper-class population; the city found itself with acres of undeveloped land on its hands. At the mayor's recommendation, these lands were offered for sale at public auction, but even by 1870 the price was not moving fast enough for the city officials. Mayor Smith urged a change in the policy of restricting South End settlement to people of wealth only. "Mechanics of limited means," he argued, "who have not credit on small resources, have a direct claim to indulgence beyond all others." The city then established more favorable loan terms and began to sell the land, preparing the way for a lower-class invasion of the South End. This deflation of prices was a deliberate, positive act of volition on the part of the city; its result was a complete deterioration in the South End's prestige value.

Thus, when Columbus Avenue was laid out in 1870, it was built with cheaper houses than those of earlier construction in the South End. Portions of the South End became middle-class and lower-class neighborhoods.

NO
PARKING
ANY TIME

Their lower prestige value spread to other parts of the district. Property values, generally an indicator of residential desirability, began to depreciate, and the panic of 1873 led to foreclosures on many of the cheaper dwellings which had been heavily mortgaged. These properties were dumped on the real estate market for whatever they could command. Beginning in 1870, and progressing more rapidly during succeeding years, the poor moved in and the rich moved out. They began to leave for the Back Bay or the country, and the heyday of the South End was over almost before it began. By 1885 the transformation of the area into a district of rooming houses was almost complete. The fine, single-family dwellings filled with lodgers or were converted into inconvenient flats. Private squares, once perfectly kept up by those who lived around them, fell into neglect. The population was transient and cared little about its temporary environment.

The In-Fill Housing Project was first tried in the South End. This is a program dependent on the city aggregating enough single lots so that the same economies of multiple housing can apply. This first program called for 200 units spread in various parts of the city. The prototype was built in the South End, but the program did not get much further. Problems came from a number of places: funds became short, zoning regulations needed to be changed, and in several instances there was strong community opposition when they saw that "new families" could be inserted into their existing community patterns. There is still substantial support for such a program, and the hope is that these obstacles can eventually be overcome.

The physical plan of the South End still has many built-in problems. The main avenues connecting Boston and Roxbury have little to do with the small community streets that cross them. Whether the new highway system will change this by altering the traditional traffic patterns is yet to be seen. But this same new highway system also has inherent problems. Early endeavors to connect the South End with the city center as well as the Back Bay were shown to be complete failures as the South End became more and more irrevocably cut off from the rest of the city by a formidable ring of depressed railroads and express highway connectors and bypasses. At the moment only major air rights projects over these roadways will heal the urban wounds.

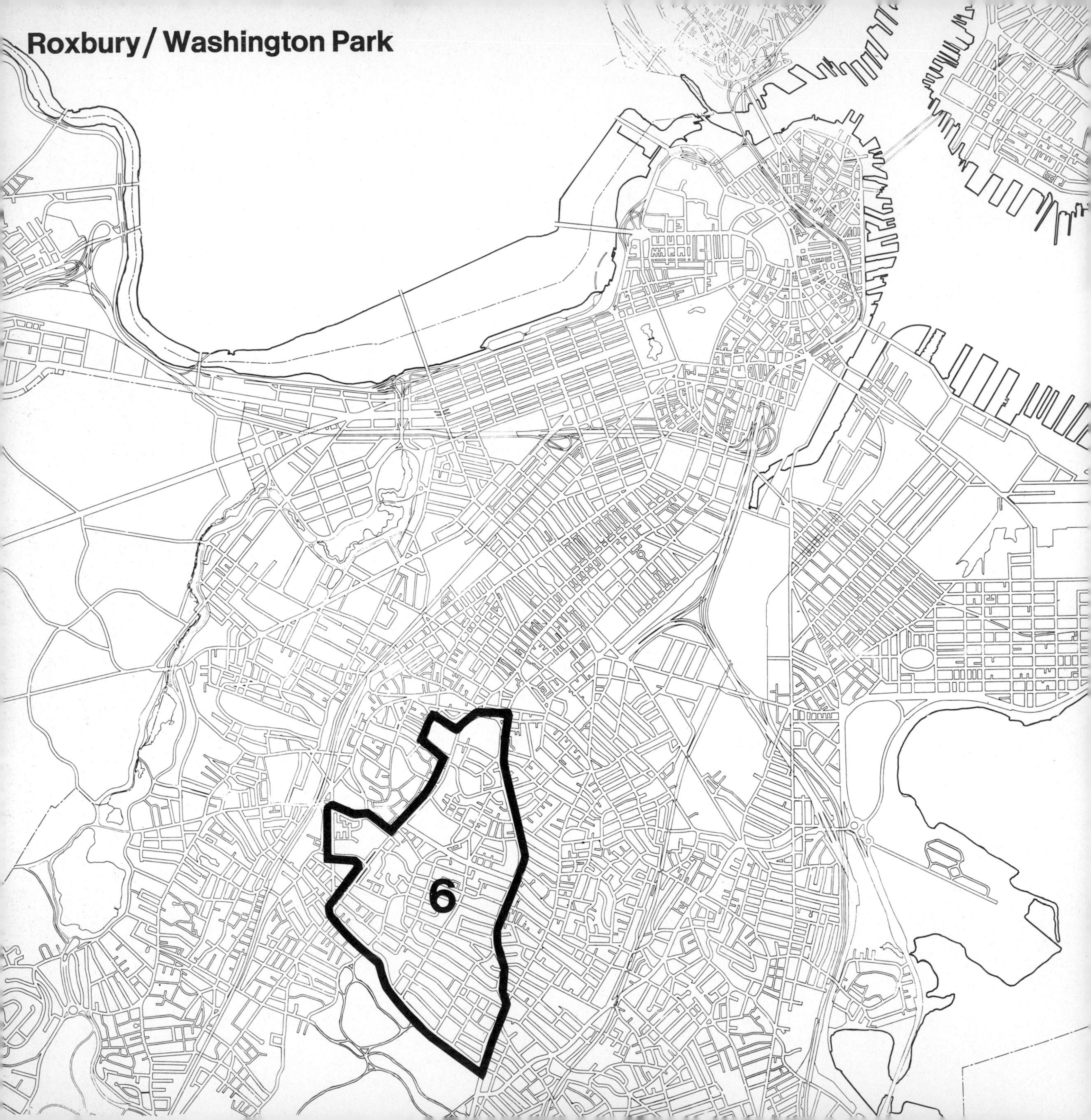
Roxbury / Washington Park
6

11
9
12
10
lambert
avenue
guild
street
8
ritchie
street
marcella
street
avenue
columbus
4
academy
road
washington
park
boulevard
street
6
dimock
street
7
5
2
1
washington
13
walnut
avenue
columbus
avenue
3
seaver
street
warren
street

Roxbury/Washington Park

1. ▶ YMCA—Washington Park
Warren Street and Washington Park Boulevard
The Architects Collaborative; 1965

2. Marksdale Gardens I
Humboldt Avenue and Townsend Street
Associated Architect and Engineer; 1964

3. Franklin Park
Frederick Law Olmsted; 1886

4. Academy Homes I
Columbus Avenue and Ritchie Street
Carl Koch & Associates; 1966

5. ▶ Academy Homes II
Washington and Dimock Streets
Carl Koch & Associates; 1968

◀ 6 Charlame II
Humboldt and Walnut Avenues
Bedar and Alpers; 1967

◀ 7. Housing for the Elderly
Boston Housing Authority
280 Washington Park Boulevard
Freeman/Flansburgh Associates; 1965

◀ 8. Warren Gardens (housing)
Warren Street and Walnut Avenue
Hugh Stubbins & Associates/
Ashley Myer & Associates; 1969

9. Shirley-Eustis House
Shirley Street
Remodeled: James Ballou; 1970

10. ▶ Boys Club of Boston
Warren and Cliff Streets
The Architects Collaborative; 1968

11. Police Station (Districts 9 and 10)
Roxbury Civic Center
Dudley and Warren Streets
Roxbury Civic Center Associates (Kallman & McKinnell and Hoyle, Doran & Berry); 1971

12. Roxbury District Courthouse
Roxbury Civic Center

13. ▶ Unity Bank & Trust Company (renovation)
416 Warren Street
Stull Associates; 1968

Roxbury/Washington Park

Roxbury is too large and complicated an area to deal with in any single-minded, simplistic sense. It encompasses the worst ghetto area in Boston and some of the noblest houses in a solid middle-class neighborhood. It has one of the best-designed parks in America and some streets that remind one of the bombed cities of Europe after the Second World War. Its people are alienated on the one hand and so motivated on the other that they can form their own bank when no one else will finance their projects. Like many such neighborhoods across America, Roxbury is in a state of transition. Its people are tired of being pushed from one undesirable, overcrowded, uninhabitable tenement to another; they have stayed and are fighting to form their own community, sometimes with outside government help, sometimes through self-help, sometimes through the Model City program. But stay they will in what was once one of the finest parts of the Boston area.

Settled in 1630, for many years the town consisted of one street, because fear of Indian attack caused the founding fathers to order all settlers to live within one half mile of the central meeting house. The Neck to Boston, always of special importance to the inhabitants of Roxbury who depended upon goods being brought across its desolate path, was the scene of tragedy and treachery. Many travelers who lost their way froze to death on the marshes; many were robbed or beaten.

Two decades brought little change in the Roxbury way of life. The Neck was fenced in, and eventually, in 1754, an attempt was made to pave and keep it in good repair. In 1793 it was formally laid out as a street, and by the close of the revolutionary war it became a fashionable spot to stroll or drive. Roxbury's female residents could, for the first time, walk safely to Boston and back, and trade between the two independent towns increased dramatically. The Neck grew in popularity, and early in the nineteenth century stage coaches traveled the Boston-Roxbury route

Barton's
SHOES
ROYCE
SHOP
WOOLWORTHS
STORES

"I am a REVOLUTIONARY"
BLACK STUDIES
L CONFERENCE
FOR A
ED FRONT
GAINST
ASCISM
In Resolution
COMMUNITY CONT OL OF FASCIST PIG POLICE
OAKLAND, CALIFORNIA
FRI, SAT AND SUN JULY 18, 19 & 20
FOR ANY INDIVIDUAL AND ESPECIAL
REPS . OF ALL PROLETARIAN TYPE
OR ANY GROUP OR ORG WHO STAND
AGAINST FASCISM IN AMERICA.
CALLED BY THE BLACK PANTHER PARTY & INT'L LIBERATION SCHOOL.
THE AMERICAN PEOPLE AND BLACK PEOPLE
IN PARTICULAR MUST RECOGNIZE FASCISM
FOR WHAT IT IS: THE DEMAGOGIC (LYING)
POLITICIAN; THE AVERICIOUS (GREEDY
EXPLOITING) BUSINESSMAN; AND THE
FASCIST PIG COPS.
BLACK PANTHER NATIONAL HEADQUARTS
OFFICE IS CHECK IN CENTER FOR THE
U.F.A.F. CONFERENCE.
3106 SHATTUCK AVE ,

once every two hours. By 1826 coaches ran every hour, and Roxbury, a separate and fairly self-sufficient entity for two hundred years, began to entertain thoughts of pledging its allegiance to Boston for mutual benefit. Coach service to Roxbury, nine cents each way, made the area look promising as a residential suburb for wealthy Bostonians, many of whom had summer houses in the area already. Building boomed in expectation of a migration of prosperous, upper-class citizens. There was a migration, but it was to the newly filled Back Bay, not to the stately homes standing ready in Roxbury.

The 1850's heralded the influx of Irish immigrants into Roxbury, a population flow that continued for twenty years. Boston annexed Roxbury in 1868, reinforcing the ties between the city and its suburb. Workers found that they could not afford the high Boston rents and looked here for lodging where good houses, through neglect and lack of market, were available at low rents and provided room for growing families.

Before the turn of the century, two other ethnic groups had entered the community in large numbers: Jews and Blacks. The predominance of Irish families went unchallenged, but the population was a constantly shifting one. Transience and neglect of buildings combined to drain the area of whatever respectability it once had. In 1914, the authors of *The Zone of Emergence* wrote about Roxbury: "One is constantly coming upon half improved streets, boarded-up factories, tumble-down buildings, shoddy dwellings inhabited by careless tenants, a dull monotony of tenements broken by certain streets of utterly unindividualized cottage houses. This condition is redeemed to some extent by the fact that there is still vacant land near some of the worst tenement blocks, that many of the cottage houses have yards, and in a few exceptional cases, gardens; and that compared with . . . downtown . . . the streets are relatively quiet and free from traffic; that the several playgrounds and parks afford generous play space for children; that excellent schools care for the

$50.00 Reward
for information leading to the arrest and conviction of anyone caught damaging or defacing this property.
POLICE TAKE NOTICE
CGC
AMERICAN LEGION
ROXBURY POST № 44
THE PIGS ARE GONNA CATCH HELL
THE REVOLUTION HAS COME

boys and girls . . . the day is not far off when the vacant land will be built upon, and land and room congestion will come close to duplicating the conditions found in the downtown wards."

By the 1930's Jewish and Black populations were pushing out the Irish; gradually the face of Roxbury had changed from the quiet Yankee town of the early nineteenth century to the twentieth-century world of tenements, crowding, and squalor. When the Jews prospered at all, they moved off to adjacent areas —Dorchester, for one—and eventually none but the poorest of their group were left. Striking evidence of the switch to Black predominance in the area is to be found in the Washington Park District: in 1950 its population was two-thirds white; in 1964 it was almost totally Black.

The Washington Park Urban Renewal Area was comprised of two neighborhoods: in the first, 25 percent of the housing was considered unsalvageable, and all but 1 percent of the rest needed rehabilitation; the second, near Roxbury's large, neglected Franklin Park, was the home of almost all of the upper-income Black families. In 1960 the Urban Renewal Program started with the enthusiastic cooperation of the area's community leaders. Residents were less convinced as the project presented enormous problems of family relocation, need of money for rehabilitation, and higher rents in whatever government-financed housing was built. Statistics are kept on the area as a means of evaluating it. What isn't kept track of is the people who live in the area. When it is shown that the crime rate has gone down, average income has gone up, school grades completed has gone up, etc., it appears that the Renewal Program has been a great success. In many instances, however, what has happened is that the low economic level of the original residents has forced them out of the higher rent area that resulted from renewal, and they and their associated problems have been forced into another district.

DIMOCK ST

There can be no quarrel that urban renewal is one mechanism for bringing positive change and improvement to Roxbury. Still, there are questions to be raised in an Urban Renewal Area that is an isolated island in the middle of a ghetto; where from opposite sides of a street, pre- and post-renewal Roxbury stares at itself in amazement, unable to recognize its own reflection; where urban renewal stops short, drawing to a halt at one street corner and ignoring what stands opposite. The questions go to the heart of the concept of a "new Boston." Isolating and enshrining government within its own symbol —new City Hall—is making evident the almost bottomless chasm between "government as establishment" and the Black "home turf" of Roxbury. We can make stop-gap measures to provide the basic necessities of life, but in the long run some recognition of the right to "quality of life" must become the central issue.

Cambridge
7

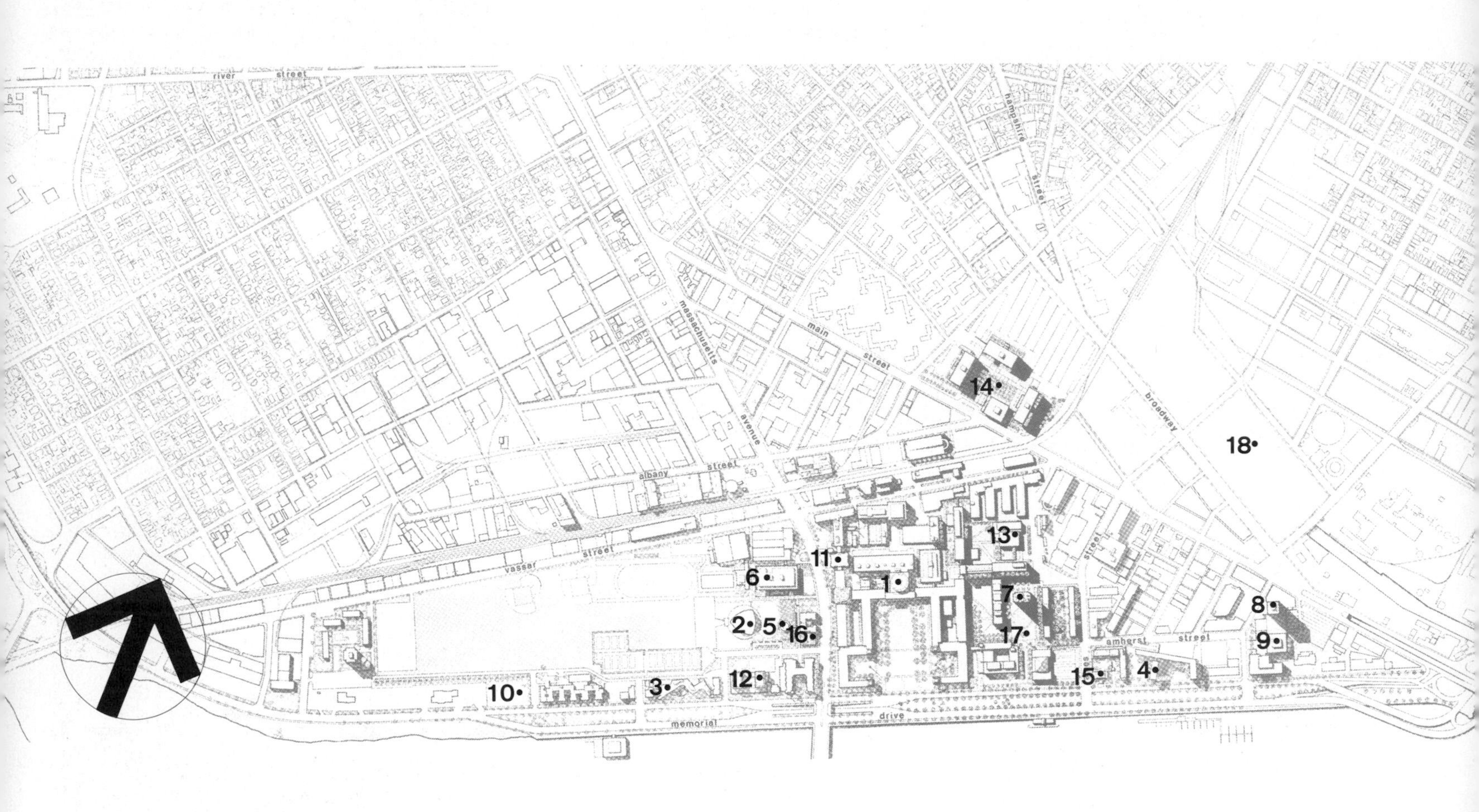

river street
hampshire street
massachusetts avenue
main street
broadway
albany street
vassar street
street
amherst street
memorial drive
1
2
3
4
5
6
7
8
9
10
11
12
13
14
15
16
17
18

Cambridge

Massachusetts Institute of Technology

◀ 1. Maclaurin Buildings
Welles Bosworth; 1913

2. ▶ Kresge Auditorium
Eero Saarinen; 1955

3. ▶ Baker House (undergraduate housing)
362 Memorial Drive
Alvar Aalto with Perry, Shaw & Hepburn; 1947–49

4. ▶ Eastgate Apartments
100 Memorial Drive
Brown, DeMars, Kennedy, Koch & Rapson; 1949

◀ 5. M.I.T. Chapel
Eero Saarinen; 1955

6. ▶ Julius Adams Stratton Building (student union)
84 Massachusetts Avenue
Eduardo Catalano with Brannen & Shimamoto; 1963

◀ 7. Green Building (earth sciences)
McDermott Court
I. M. Pei & Associates; 1964

8. ▶ Eastgate Married Students Housing
Wadsworth and Main Streets
Eduardo Catalano; 1966

◀ 9. Grover M. Hermann Building
30 Wadsworth Street
Eduardo Catalano; 1964

10. Frank S. MacGregor House
(undergraduate housing)
450 Memorial Drive
The Architects Collaborative and
Pietro Belluschi; 1970

◀ 11. Center for Advanced Engineering Studies
105 Massachusetts Avenue
Skidmore, Owings & Merrill; 1966

◀ 12. McCormick Hall (women's housing)
320 Memorial Drive
Anderson, Beckwith & Haible; 1967

13. ▶ Alumni Swimming Pool
Anderson & Beckwith; 1940

14. ▶ Technology Square
Main Street
Cabot, Cabot & Forbes; 1963–64
Pietro Belluschi and Eduardo Catalano;
1965–66

15. President's House
111 Memorial Drive
Welles Bosworth; 1917

◀ 16. Center for Advanced Visual Studies
40 Massachusetts Avenue
Marvin E. Goody & John M. Clancy; 1967

17. La Grande Voile (stabile)
Alexander Calder; 1966

18. N.A.S.A.
Tower: Edward Durrell Stone; 1970
Optics and Guidance Laboratories:
The Architects Collaborative; 1970

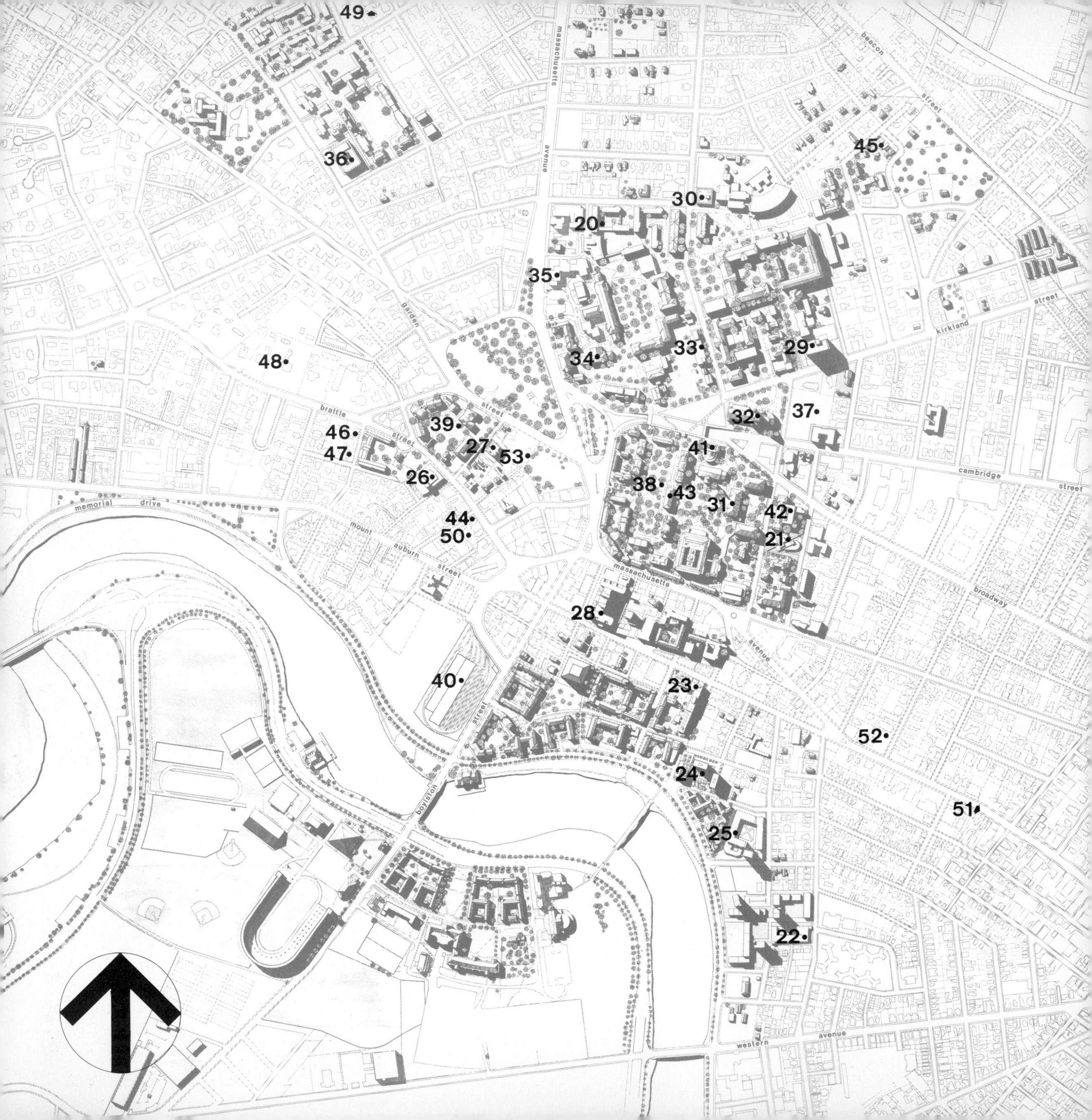
49
36
45
massachusetts
avenue
beacon
street
30
20
35
kirkland
street
garden
48
34
33
29
brattle
street
39
32
37
46
47
27
53
41
cambridge
street
26
38
43
31
42
memorial
drive
44
50
21
mount
auburn
street
massachusetts
broadway
28
avenue
40
23
street
52
boylston
24
51
25
22
western
avenue

Harvard University

20. ▶ Harvard Graduate Center
14 Everett Street
The Architects Collaborative; 1949

21. ▶ Carpenter Center for the Visual Arts
19 Prescott Street
Le Corbusier with Sert, Jackson & Gourley; 1963

◀ **22.** Peabody Terrace (married students housing)
900 Memorial Drive
Sert, Jackson & Gourley; 1963

23. ▶ Quincy House
58 Plympton Street
Shepley, Bulfinch, Richardson & Abbott; 1958

◀ **24.** Leverett House Library and Towers
Memorial Drive and De Wolfe Street
Shepley, Bulfinch, Richardson & Abbott; 1959

25. Mather House
Cowperthwaite Street
Shepley, Bulfinch, Richardson & Abbott; 1970

26. ▶ Loeb Drama Center
64 Brattle Street
Hugh Stubbins & Associates; 1959

◀ **27.** Graduate School of Education
6 Appian Way
Caudill, Rowlett & Scott; 1965

28. ▶ Holyoke Center
1350 Massachusetts Avenue
Sert, Jackson & Gourley; 1961–65

29. ▶ William James Hall
33 Kirkland Street
Minoru Yamasaki and Associates; 1962

◀ **30.** Engineering Sciences Building
40 Oxford Street
Minoru Yamasaki and Associates; 1962

◀ **31.** Sever Hall
Harvard Yard
H. H. Richardson; 1880

◀ **32.** Memorial Hall
Cambridge and Quincy Streets
Ware and Van Brunt; 1870

33. Gordon McKay Laboratory
9 Oxford Street
Shepley, Bulfinch, Richardson & Abbott; 1952

34. ▶ Austin Hall
6 Holmes Place
H. H. Richardson; 1881

◀ **35.** Law School Faculty Office Building
Massachusetts Avenue
Benjamin Thompson & Associates; 1967

36. Hilles Library, Radcliffe College
59 Shepard Street
Harrison & Abramovitz; 1965
▶ (picture: opposite page, top right)

37. Gund Hall (Graduate School of Design)
Quincy and Cambridge Streets
John Andrews/Anderson/Baldwin; 1971

38. Old Harvard Yard

Massachusetts Hall
1720

Holden Chapel
1744

Hollis Hall
Thomas Dawes; 1763

Harvard Hall
Gov. Francis Bernard and Thomas Dawes; 1766; additions: 1842, 1870

Stoughton Hall
Charles Bulfinch, Thomas Dawes; 1805

Holworthy Hall
Laommi Baldwin; 1812

Boylston Hall
Schultze & Schoen; 1856
The Architects Collaborative; 1959

Grays Hall
N. J. Bradlee; 1863

Mathews Hall
Peabody and Stearns; 1870

Thayer Hall
Ryder & Harris; 1870

Weld Hall
William Robert Ware; 1871

39. Old Radcliffe Yard

40. J. F. Kennedy Memorial Library
I. M. Pei & Partners; 197-

41. Hunt Hall (originally Fogg Museum of Art)
Richard Morris Hunt; 1893

42. Fogg Museum of Art
Coolidge, Shepley, Bulfinch & Abbott; 1925

43. University Hall
Charles Bulfinch; 1813–15

Other Cambridge Buildings

44. ▶ Design Research Inc.
48 Brattle Street
Benjamin Thompson & Associates; 1969

45. ▶ José Luis Sert Residence
64 Francis Avenue
José Luis Sert; 1957

46. M. F. Stoughton House
90 Brattle Street
H. H. Richardson; 1883

47. 9 Ash Street
Philip Johnson; 1941

48. Vassal House (Longfellow House)
105 Brattle Street
1759

49. 1 Mount Pleasant Street
Paul Rudolph; 1957

◀ **50.** The Architects Collaborative Office Building
46 Brattle Street
The Architects Collaborative; 1966

51. ▶ New England Gas and Electric Association
130 Austin Street
Sert, Jackson & Gourley; 1960

◀ **52.** 1033 Massachusetts Avenue
Hugh Stubbins & Associates; 1969

◀ **53.** Christ Church
Zero Garden Street
Peter Harrison; 1759

GELOTTE CAMERAS
CRIMSON CAMERAS
CRIMSON CAMERA EXCH. KODAKS
ONE HOUR PARKING
NO PARKING
Harvard BARBE
ONE WAY
HARVARD TRAVEL SERVICE INC.
Bolter Company MEN'S APPAREL
Hayes Bickford's RESTAURANT
XEROX

CAMBRIDGE

At last count, there were at least sixty colleges and universities in the Greater Boston area. More than just a cultural resource, they have become one of the prime factors in the region's new economic growth. Research and development corporations and associated industries have flocked to the area to tap the universities' brainpower. At the core of this academic community lie the two universities along the Cambridge side of the Charles River: Harvard and M.I.T. These two campuses have been growing at a spectacular rate, and their changing scale has made them major landmarks along the river.

Cambridge was originally called New Towne, founded in 1630 approximately at the site of what is today Harvard Square. As early as 1635 the village made provision for a public ferry to Boston, which operated until 1662 when it was replaced by a bridge.

In 1636 the colonial government announced its intention of establishing a college in the village, and New Towne's name was changed to Cambridge, in honor of the English university town. When John Harvard died in 1693 and left his library and half his estate to the fledgling college, it took his name in an expression of gratitude. The earliest Harvard buildings were clustered around the center of what is now old Harvard Yard, so named to distinguish it from an adjacent cow yard.

The revolutionary war brought no battles to Cambridge, but it was the center of much planning and quartering of troops on the Inman and Foxcroft estates. After the Battle of Bunker Hill, these two Tory sympathizers accommodated the tents of nearly four thousand soldiers on their grounds; the estates did not revert to their owners until 1783. After the Revolution, several of the large land holdings around Harvard were broken up, and new roadways were opened to other villages near by. Two other settlements, East Cambridge and Cambridgeport, were also growing rapidly. Each was separated from the Harvard Square community by open fields and salt marshes; each was the scene of great industrial activity. As transportation improved, these two villages became potential suburbs of the rapidly growing city of Boston.

Cambridgeport had hopes of becoming a major deep-water port, and a system of canals was ambitiously built. The Embargo Act of 1807 and the War of 1812 put an end to its shipping future, but the community continued to prosper as an industrial center, as did East Cambridge. The construction of a new bridge made possible a direct, convenient route for horse-drawn streetcars from Boston into Harvard and Central Squares, and with it came the demand for additional housing. Harvard Square, which had maintained its attraction as a cultural and professional center, and the area known as Mid-Cambridge—the open fields that had separated the three villages—developed rapidly into highly desirable residential neighborhoods.

By the middle of the century the remaining large country estates were being subdivided into lots to meet the demands for housing, and Harvard University was able to buy much of the new land at that time. This was to be a significant factor in the growth pattern of Cambridge in later years. By the end of the nineteenth century, the Harvard Square, East Cambridge, and Cambridgeport sections had gradually merged, and building had extended into the hitherto uninhabited region of North and West Cambridge. In the 1880's a concerted effort was made to clean up the waterfront. By 1910 the Charles River tidal dam was completed and turned the river from one of harbor tides and mud flats into a pleasant body of fresh water. The Charles River Embankment Company was formed to fill land along the river and construct an esplanade.

Although the land use pattern in Cambridge was firmly established by the First World War, building activity slumped from that time until the end of World War II. The 1950's saw new construction and a revitalization of Cambridge architecture. The architecture departments of both Harvard and M.I.T. had attracted many of the profession who chose to live and work in Cambridge, and their influence was felt in both institutional and private design. M.I.T.'s W. W. Wurster, as head of the country's oldest architectural school, and Harvard's Walter Gropius brought about a new architectural education program which produced many of America's outstanding architects and teachers.

The campuses of Harvard and M.I.T. are antithetical in plan: Harvard has never had a master plan but has grown organically through need and a set of governing "concepts" on such matters as the selection and utilization of sites, the height and bulk of buildings, and especially the continuity of Harvard's green spaces. An anonymous observer called Harvard "a collection of departments held together by allegiance to a central heating plant." Each academic unit has its own budget and often its own endowments, so that development has been sporadic and individual. M.I.T.'s master plan has been based on its philosophy of the interdisciplinary quality of science and technology and a maximum of connection between and flexibility within buildings. M.I.T. has often put one architectural firm in charge of a whole portion of its campus, producing a more unified design than found at Harvard. Paradoxically, José Luis Sert, while Dean of Harvard's Graduate School of Design, is quoted as saying that the urban campus "should set an example of good planning and good design. It is, in a way, a micro-city and its urbanity is the expression of a better, more civilized way of life."

The same economic and structural problems that are forcing a scale change in Boston are bringing about the decision to build higher

SEVER HALL

ONE
ONE HOUR PARKING
8AM - 6PM
EX SUN
TOW AWAY ZONE
NO STANDING
ALEXANDER NEVSKY
A. CAHAL

buildings on the Cambridge side of the river. These new towers have made the universities much more evident than did their low buildings before the 1950's. But to the inhabitants of Cambridge, many of whom are totally unconnected with either university, Harvard and M.I.T. stand as superpowers, able to take over homes, raise rents, destroy historic buildings, and sit tax-free in a world of spiraling inflation. The feeling is that the enormous demand for housing created by those brought to Cambridge by the universities makes single-family dwellings increasingly less practical, and many of the fine old residential streets have disappeared under high-rise apartment buildings and parking lots.

From the viewpoint of the universities, this time-honored tradition of conflict between town and gown is a canard. Land held by the universities makes up a small percentage of the available land area in Cambridge: only 350 acres (8.8 percent) of the total 4000 acres are given to higher education. The story of a tax-free institution is also untrue; all responsible institutions have recognized their role in cooperating with the city, and Harvard and M.I.T. turn out to be the largest taxpayers in Cambridge—sometimes paying "in lieu of taxes," sometimes paying for specific services such as the building of roads and fire houses, and sometimes giving direct assistance. In one of the latest City Reports Harvard and M.I.T. were recorded as each having paid over $500,000 in lieu of taxes. The next largest taxpayer in the city paid a total of $276,000. Finally, town-gown antipathy seems more a question of lack of communication than of actual opposition. Both universities have tried to establish long-lasting community relationship programs. The Cambridge Corporation is an action group funded by the two universities and was responsible to a large degree for the written program for the Cambridge Model Cities proposal. There can be no doubt that the universities have a profound effect on the city, both intellectually and financially. M.I.T. alone has a supporting staff larger than its student body. But the issue that has been raised repeatedly is the right of the universi-

ties, or for that matter any large corporation or agency, to displace anyone at all. The same question was brought up when the Inner Belt Highway was planned to go through a section of Cambridge, thereby displacing some three hundred families. That project has been at least momentarily stopped, but it was of interest that some of the same people who were responsible for stopping the road offered an alternative proposal for taking the road down the river bank, where it would not displace anyone; it would take away a major recreational area—one of the only greenways in a densely populated city—but it would not displace anyone.

Perhaps the town-gown relationship was best summed up in an article in *Architectural Forum:* "Where the university takes over, the area becomes semi-public, and patterns of use change. The more leisurely pace of family life is replaced by the bustle of students rushing between classes; when night comes, the domestic warmth of house lights is replaced by darkness and isolation. At the same time, the intimate scale and rhythm of small houses and gardens gives way to the more ponderous masses of large buildings, and to the impersonality of public planting."

Places of particular interest outside the immediate Boston area

Towns

North
Marblehead, Old Town and Harbor
Salem, Old Town
Rockport and Gloucester

West
Shirley Village Green
Amherst and Hadler
Concord
Lexington, Battle Green

South
Cohasset
Hingham and Scituate
Duxbury
Plymouth
Sandwich, Cape Cod
Chatham, Cape Cod
Wychmere Harbor, Cape Cod

Museums

Boston Area
Museum of Science, Boston
Children's Museum, Jamaica Plain
Fogg Art Museum, Cambridge
Antique Auto Museum, Larz Andersen Park, Brookline

North
Addison Gallery of American Art, Andover
Merrimack Valley Textile Museum, N. Andover
Peabody Museum, Salem
Antiquarian Museum, Concord

West
Wellesley College Art Museum, Wellesley
Worcester Art Museum, Worcester

South
Whaling Museum, New Bedford
Pilgrim Hall, Plymouth

Outdoor Museums

Boston Area
Saugus Iron Works, Saugus

North
Pioneer Village, Salem
Strawberry Banke, Portsmouth, N.H.

West
Minuteman National Park, Concord
Sleepy Hollow, Concord
Old Sturbridge Village, Sturbridge
Old Deerfield Village, Deerfield
Hancock Shaker Village, near Pittsfield

South
Plymouth Plantation, Plymouth

Historic Houses

Boston Area
Brattle Street, Cambridge
42, 55, corner Ash Street, 145, 153, 159, 175
Warren Street and Goddard Avenue, Brookline
Fairbanks House, Dedham

North
Royal House, Medford
Jeremiah Lee Mansion, Marblehead
Balch, Cabot, Hale Houses, Beverley
Beaufor House, Gloucester
Hammond Castle, Gloucester
Short, Wett-Ilsely, Tristram Coffin Houses, Newbury
Federal, Essex, and Chestnut Streets, Salem

West
Emerson House, Concord
Old Manse (Hawthorne), Concord
Orchard House (Alcott), Concord
Buchman & Munroe Taverns, Lexington
Hancock Clarke House, Lexington

South
Adams Houses, Quincy
John Alden House, Duxbury
Winslow House, Marshfield
Antiquarian House, Plymouth
Harlow Old Fort House
Jabez Howland House, Plymouth
Richard Sparrow House, Plymouth
Spooner House, Plymouth

Bibliography

Books

American Federation of Arts, New York, and The Institute of Contemporary Art, Boston. *The Cultural Resources of Boston.* New York, 1965.

American Society of Landscape Architects. *Transactions.* Harrisburg, Pennsylvania, 1912.

Bunting, Bainbridge. *Houses of Boston's Back Bay.* Cambridge, Massachusetts: The Belknap Press of Harvard University Press, 1967.

Cambridge Historical Commission. *Survey of Architectural History in Cambridge: Report One: East Cambridge.* Cambridge, Massachusetts, 1965.

Cambridge Historical Commission. *Survey of Architectural History in Cambridge: Report Two: Mid-Cambridge.* Cambridge, Massachusetts, 1967.

Fabos, Julius Gy., Milde, Gordon T., and Weinmayr, V. Michael. *Frederick Law Olmsted, Sr. Founder of Landscape Architecture in America.* Amherst, Massachusetts: The University of Massachusetts Press, 1968.

Firey, Walter. *Land Use in Central Boston.* Cambridge, Massachusetts: Harvard University Press, 1947.

Goody, Marvin E., and Walsh, Robert P., eds. *Boston Society of Architects 1867–1967.* Boston: *The Boston Society of Architects,* 1967.

Handlin, Oscar. *Boston's Immigrants 1790–1865.* Cambridge, Massachusetts: Harvard University Press, 1941.

Hitchcock, Henry-Russell. *A Guide to Boston Architecture 1637–1954.* New York: Reinhold, 1954.

Rettig, Robert Bell. *Guide to Cambridge Architecture: Ten Walking Tours.* Cambridge, Massachusetts: The M.I.T. Press, 1969.

Rodwin, Lloyd. *Housing and Economic Progress.* Cambridge, Massachusetts: Harvard University Press and The Technology Press, 1961.

Shackleton, Robert. *The Book of Boston.* Philadelphia: The Penn Publishing Company, 1917.

Shurtleff, Nathaniel B. *A Topographical and Historical Description of Boston.* Boston: Published by Order of the City Council, 1890.

Warner, Sam B., Jr. *Streetcar Suburbs: The Process of Growth in Boston 1870–1900.* Cambridge, Massachusetts: Harvard University Press and The M.I.T. Press, 1962.

Weston, George F., Jr. *Boston Ways, High, By and Folk.* Boston: Beacon Press, 1957.

Whitehill, Walter M. *Boston—A Topographical History.* 2nd ed. Cambridge, Massachusetts: The Belknap Press of Harvard University Press, 1968.

Woods, Robert A., ed. *The City Wilderness.* Cambridge, Massachusetts: The Riverside Press, 1898.

Woods, Robert A., and Kennedy, Albert J. *The Zone of Emergence.* Cambridge, Massachusetts: Harvard University Press, 1962.

Articles

"Boston." *Architectural Forum,* June, 1964, special issue.

Mumford, Lewis. "The Making of a Precedent, 1840–90." *Boston,* October, 1969, pp. 42–46.

Proceedings

Boston Architectural Center Conference. *The City as a System.* Boston, 1967–68.

Boston Architectural Center Conference. *The New John Hancock Building.* Boston, May 4, 1968.

Reports

Adams, Howard and Oppermann. *Back Bay Development Plan.* Prepared for the Boston Redevelopment Authority and the Back Bay Planning and Development Corporation, July, 1970.

Gruen, Victor, and Associates, Inc. *Boston Central Business District Planning Report.* Prepared for the Boston Redevelopment Authority and the Committee for the Central Business District, October 30, 1967.

Pillorgé, George J. *Factors that Shape the City.* Submitted for Urban Design Seminar, Graduate School of Design, Harvard University, December 20, 1960.

Rapkin, Chester. *The Seaver-Townsend Urban Renewal Area.* Prepared for the Boston Redevelopment Authority, January, 1962.

Smart, Walter L. *Diagnostic Report—Residents of the South End Urban Renewal Project.* Boston Redevelopment Authority Family Relocation Department, June, 1967.

Smith, Larry, and Company. *Land Utilization and Marketability Study.* Prepared for Boston Redevelopment Authority, January 31, 1963.

Reports (by title)

Post-War Cambridge: Report to the City Council on Post-War Plans. Frederick J. Adams, chairman. Cambridge: Office of the City Manager, 1945.

Preliminary Report on a General Plan for Boston. Thomas F. McDonough, chairman. Boston: Office of the City Planning Board, September 20, 1951.

Rehabilitation in Boston. William S. Parker, chairman. Boston: Office of the City Planning Board, November 1, 1941.

Report on a Thoroughfare Plan for Boston. Frederic H. Fay, chairman. Boston: City Planning Board, 1930.

Reports (by commission)

Boston. Chamber of Commerce. *Boston, Massachusetts.* Boston: Convention Bureau, 1928.

Boston. Housing Authority. *Supporting Documentation to the Redevelopment Plan.* Boston, September, 1955.

Boston. Metropolitan Area Planning Council. *Open Space and Recreation Program for Metropolitan Boston.* Vol. 2, *Boston Harbor,* 1967.

Committee Appointed by the President of Harvard University at the Request of the Mayor of Cambridge. *The Future Development of Harvard Square and its Neighborhood.* Cambridge, 1913.

Greater Boston Study Committee. *A Report on Downtown Boston.* Boston, May, 1959.

Massachusetts Port Authority. *Annual Report. Massport '68.* Boston: Massachusetts Port Authority, July 1, 1967–June 30, 1968.

U.S. Department of Housing and Urban Development. *Analysis of the Boston, Massachusetts, Housing Market.* Washington, D.C., October, 1967.

Photograph Credits

Introduction

1-New England Survey Service. 2-Richard Rogers. 3-Don Freeman. 4-Don Freeman. 5-Richard Rogers.

Chapter 1—Beacon Hill

7-Nanette Sexton. 9-Nanette Sexton. 10-Nanette Sexton. 11-Don Freeman. 12-Richard Rogers, Todd Stuart. 13-Richard Rogers. 14-Richard Rogers. 15-Richard Rogers, Nanette Sexton, Todd Stuart. 16-Don Freeman, Richard Rogers, Todd Stuart. 17-Richard Rogers, Todd Stuart.

Chapter 2—Back Bay/The Fenway

19-Nanette Sexton. 21-Nanette Sexton, David Hirsch (#1). 22-Nanette Sexton. 23-Nanette Sexton, Todd Stuart (#21). 24-Boston Public Library. 25-New England Aerial Survey. 26/27-Nanette Sexton. 28-Don Freeman, Nanette Sexton. 29-Don Freeman, Nanette Sexton, Todd Stuart. 30-Richard Rogers, Nanette Sexton, Todd Stuart. 31-Don Freeman, Richard Rogers, Nanette Sexton, Todd Stuart. 32-Don Freeman. 33-Don Freeman, Richard Rogers, Nanette Sexton. 34-Richard Rogers. 35-John Hancock Co. 37-Nanette Sexton. 38-Nanette Sexton. 40-Don Freeman.

Chapter 3—Central Business District/ Government Center

43-Don Freeman. 45-Nanette Sexton. 46-Nanette Sexton. 47-Nanette Sexton. 48-Nanette Sexton. 50-Nanette Sexton. 51-Nanette Sexton. 52-Nanette Sexton. 53-Nanette Sexton. 54-Nanette Sexton. 55-Todd Stuart. 56-New England Aerial Survey. 57-Don Freeman. 58-Don Freeman, Nanette Sexton. 59-Nanette Sexton.

Chapter 4—Waterfront

61-George Zimberg. 63-Nanette Sexton. 64-Nanette Sexton. 65-Richard Rogers. 66-Richard Rogers. 67-Richard Rogers. 68-Richard Rogers. 69-Richard Rogers. 96-Nanette Sexton. 97-Nanette Sexton.

Chapter 5—South End

73-Todd Stuart. 75-Don Freeman (#3), Nanette Sexton. 76-Nanette Sexton. 77-Todd Stuart. 78-Myron Miller, Todd Stuart. 79-Myron Miller, Todd Stuart. 80-Don Freeman, Nanette Sexton, Todd Stuart. 81-Todd Stuart. 82-Todd Stuart. 83-Richard Rogers.

Chapter 6—Roxbury

85-Nanette Sexton. 87-Don Freeman (#6), Nanette Sexton. 88-Nanette Sexton. 90-Don Freeman, Nanette Sexton. 91-Nanette Sexton. 92-Nanette Sexton. 93-Don Freeman. 94-Nanette Sexton. 95-Richard Rogers. 96-Nanette Sexton. 97-Nanette Sexton.

Chapter 7—Cambridge

99-Don Freeman. 101-Nanette Sexton. 102-Nanette Sexton. 103-Don Freeman. 105-Nanette Sexton. 106-Nanette Sexton. 107-Nanette Sexton. 108-Don Freeman. 110-Richard Rogers. 111-Don Freeman. 112-Don Freeman. 113-Richard Rogers. 114-Don Freeman. 115-Don Freeman.